The Work of Operating Foundations
Strategies – Instruments – Perspectives

The Work of Operating Foundations

Strategies – Instruments – Perspectives

Bertelsmann Foundation (ed.)

With contributions from:

Harvey P. Dale
Ricardo Díez-Hochleitner
Roman Herzog
Mikio Kato
Reinhard Mohn
Rüdiger Stephan
Werner Weidenfeld
Mark Wössner

Bertelsmann Foundation Publishers
Gütersloh 1997

Die Deutsche Bibliothek – CIP-Einheitsaufnahme

The **work of operating foundations** : strategies – instruments – perspectives / Bertelsmann Foundation (ed.). With contributions from: Harvey P. Dale ... - Gütersloh : Bertelsmann Foundation, 1997
ISBN 3-89204-248-9

© Bertelsmann Foundation Publishers, Gütersloh
Responsible: Dr. Roland Kaehlbrandt, Volker Then
Editors: Dr. Marita Haibach, Dr. Roland Kaehlbrandt, Volker Then
Copy editor: Brigitte Neuparth
Production editor: Sabine Klemm
Cover design: HTG Werbeagentur, Bielefeld
Cover photo: G+J Fotoservice/Phototonica, Hamburg
Typesetting: digitron GmbH, Bielefeld
Print: Fuldaer Verlagsanstalt, Fulda
ISBN 3-89204-248-9

Contents

Summary 9

Foreword 13

Introduction

Making change possible 17
Werner Weidenfeld

Objectives of an operating foundation 24
Reinhard Mohn

The responsibility of foundations

The significance of foundations in our day 35
President Roman Herzog

Foundations as guarantors of entrepreneurial
continuity and social responsibility 42
Mark Wössner

Inspiring international cooperation 48
Ricardo Díez-Hochleitner

International experiences

U.S. law affecting foundations and
their ownership of businesses 57
Harvey P. Dale

Operating foundations in Europe 69
Rüdiger Stephan

Japan's experiences with operating foundations 78
Mikio Kato

Reports from the workshops

Workshop I
Governance and strategy of foundations 89
Moderation: Joel L. Fleishman

Workshop II
Cooperation of foundations 97
Moderation: Wolfgang H. Reinicke

Workshop III
Effectiveness and legitimacy of foundations 107
Moderation: Rien van Gendt

Workshop IV
Efficiency and management of foundations 115
Moderation: Craig Kennedy

Workshop V
Community foundations 121
Moderation: Shannon E. St. John

Conclusion

The responsibility of foundations today 133
Reinhard Mohn

Annex

The authors 145

The participants 148

Theses of the Bertelsmann Foundation 155

Summary

The term "operating foundation" used in this publication refers to an institution which initiates ideas for projects in which it becomes involved. It assists in setting up and organizing the projects – from inception to implementation. Operating foundation efforts concentrate on developing efficient reform strategies for problems within society which the foundation has chosen to tackle. The work is carried out in collaboration with state and public institutions with recourse to scientific and academic expertise. Operating foundations are complemented by grantmaking foundations and by a type of foundation which combines both operative and grantmaking activities.

The efficacy of the state is declining with regard to its ability to deal with issues which have become increasingly difficult as a result of a lack of broader social consensus. At such a time, operating foundations as a concentrated form of civic commitment to society can and must work on resolving these problems in an unbiased way and on putting the solutions into effect in certain chosen areas of society. As they are not committed to one interest group in particular, it is their responsibility to take advantage of the special status they possess by asking searching or unsettling questions and exploring propositions for innovative solutions.

from: Bertelsmann Foundation (ed.)
   The Work of Operating Foundations: Strategies – Instruments – Perspectives

They must, of course, provide proof of the feasibility and usefulness of their suggestions.

Because of the influence they have in society, business corporations are obliged to assume social responsibility nowadays. Foundations are an excellent way to achieve this. When establishing a foundation, it seems self-evident that corporate policy considerations, i. e. questions of corporate continuity, are as important as social considerations – at least in the context of German jurisdiction. Furthermore, the leadership and management qualifications required for work with foundations can only be fulfilled by executives who, as a result of their professional experience, meet the conditions which are so important for foundation work in particular: creativity and the ability to solve problems.

Foundations are characterized nationally by a diversity of issues and methods, but there are also significant differences to be witnessed internationally. In the United States, for example, contrary to common belief, legislation with regard to foundations is anything but foundation-friendly. Arising from a certain distrust of the powerful American foundations, a US law was passed some 30 years ago restricting to a minimum the amount of shares a foundation is allowed to vest in a corporation. This is in sharp contrast to German legislation. Unlike their US-American counterparts which are greatly committed to socio-political issues, European foundations tend to concentrate more on projects of understanding between nations. The focus lies on bridge-building within Europe, in particular, to the Central and Eastern European states, as well as to non-European cultures. Post-war history has provided us with examples of this commitment: the contributions made by foundations and non-profit initiatives towards German-French and German-Polish relations, for example. A glance at Japanese foundations illustrates how a dominant state and an inadequate management policy can have adverse effects on foundations (foundations there are mostly run by retired government officials, not particularly open to innovation). It was only after the earthquake in Kobe in 1995 that the unwieldiness of the state became apparent and a new way of thinking developed. In the meantime, numerous small dynamic foundations and non-governmental organizations have been created which represent this new form of civic commitment.

As the foundation movement grows, questions concerning strategies and joint cooperation, foundation structure, management, legitimacy and effectiveness are becoming increasingly important. Strategically, foundations have a key role to play as pioneers of social change. They must not, however, limit themselves to simply reprehending the current state of affairs; they must become active as model-makers themselves, without, however, being used as stopgaps for the state. For strategic reasons, the globalization of political, economic, social and cultural affairs requires that foundations all over the world cooperate. Only in this way can these organizations – the funding of which is limited – combine their forces and support in a concerted effort much needed transformation processes. Successful cooperation demands a clear division of lines of authority, rights, responsibilities and rewards. Concerning foundation structure, the US experience with regard to corporate foundations illustrates that it is advisable to transfer voting rights to trust companies experienced in foundation work, to define methods for properly selecting foundation staff and to set up clear guidelines as to expenditure. The statutes should be formulated in such a way that no objectives are defined which are too specific or upon which a time limit has been set. This would enable foundations to adjust to the changing needs of society. In order to secure the effectiveness of foundation work, the management of the foundation is advised to define assessment criteria for results achieved. Bureaucratic formalities, however, should be avoided as these can hinder foundations in their willingness to take risks. Efficiency and the capacity for innovation are contingent upon, among other things, the quality of the executive staff, performance-oriented management, open and flexible working conditions, clear targets, an appropriate choice of projects, evaluation and cooperation. The effectiveness, i. e. the powerful impact a foundation can have, is based on clear objectives, systematic methods of work planned out well in advance and the ability of the organization to become part of a learning process. Also important are performance orientation, the willingness to experiment with different processes and the ability to communicate the themes and results. Foundations can counter doubts as to the legitimacy of their actions by explaining the non-profit advantages resulting from their political neutrality, by developing a code of conduct for foundations, by defining a clear task program and by publishing the results of their work, thereby providing the public with a clear picture of foundation activities.

In connection with the debate concerning the imminent loss of social unity in pluralistic societies, there is one type of foundation – still a novelty in Germany – which is of special interest: the community foundation. It is a locally or regionally committed foundation which, benefiting from local citizens' attachment to their communities, mobilizes charitable capital and thereby establishes links between the individual and the community. These foundations, which make up the largest, fastest growing type of foundation in the United States, see themselves as coordinators and catalysts for private social initiatives scattered about the region. They tap resources, provide donors with services for investing their contributions and, in their role as promoting institutions, react quickly and unbureaucratically to the changing needs of the community. This is a model which could be very relevant for Germany in view of the limits of the welfare state and the decline in the ability to develop a sense of community and to reach social consensus.

Foreword

It must be clear to anyone dealing with the rapid changes in the economy, politics and culture that many of society's problems can no longer be viewed nor solved at the national level. Foundations, as agents of social change, have the task of adjusting their methods of work and concepts of problem-solving to these new developments. An exchange of ideas at an international level and interdisciplinary cooperation are required.

It was for this reason that the Bertelsmann Foundation invited executives from foundations all around the world to take part in the symposium on the work of operating foundations, "Strategies – Instruments – Perspectives" in spring 1996. The conference took place on the occasion of the 75th birthday of the founder, Reinhard Mohn, who had made this symposium his birthday wish. Professor Dr. Werner Weidenfeld, Member of the Board of Directors of the Bertelsmann Foundation, was in charge of the event.

Three aims were pursued in this endeavor: to exchange ideas on methods and models of foundation work in an international comparison, to anchor foundation philosophy in the public mind and increase its popularity. In addition, German foundations were provided with the possibility of participating in an exchange of experience and know-how of leading foundations from around the world. Chairmen, presidents, foundation experts, executives and managing staff members from over 40 foundations took part in the conference to discuss strategies, techniques and models of foundation work.

In the following book we have attempted to document the results of this productive international forum. In addition to the speeches presented at the symposium which we have included in this volume, we have also summarized the discussions which took place in the more thematically-focused workshops. Many concrete approaches to the everyday working of foundations are formulated in this book which will be of great interest to the entire foundation landscape.

We hope that this documentation will contribute to the far-reaching impulses resulting from the forum. Spurred on by the encouragement received from the symposium participants, the Bertelsmann Foundation has seized the occasion to strengthen its own commitment to foundation development.

Roland Kaehlbrandt
Volker Then

Introduction

Making change possible

Werner Weidenfeld

There cannot be enough said about the importance of foundations in our modern day. Foundations are a basic component of our *civil society* and the keystone of democratic order.

With these considerations in mind, the Bertelsmann Foundation initiated this forum in order to exchange ideas on the work of operating foundations. Just one glance at the audience reveals that we are in the midst of an international summit of the operating foundation world. We can look forward to the inspiration, ideas and impetus that will emerge from such a conference, in which presidents and members of the board of more than 40 operating foundations from 11 countries are participating.

The necessity for optimizing the work of operating foundations

Habitually in this room, in the course of the daily activities of the Bertelsmann Foundation, conferences, meetings and workshops are held dealing with problem-solving concepts in international conflicts, the ethics of journalism, the improvement of self-administration in local government, the future of labor relations and much more. These are the topics which we grapple with daily – operatively. We ascertain the need for action in problem areas, we develop criteria and strategies for problem-solving and we then attempt to implement the strategies.

By focusing our attention on optimizing the work of operating foundations, it may look as if we are jumping ahead of ourselves. In reality, we are only shifting the emphasis. Improving foundation work represents part of the overall response to the numerous challenges within our social systems presented to us daily. In the past and present day, we have often seen societies, under great pressure from the difficulties they encounter, become rigid and restrictive and refuse to institute reforms; they attempt to avoid confronting the difficulties they find themselves in. It is natural that in such situations we look towards independent organizations to provide new impetus. An operating foundation, as a center for creativity, holds a key position today in the political culture of our society. As its social importance increases, however, the number of questions which arise about foundational work also increase. Questions emerge concerning a foundation's responsibility to society, its effectiveness, the accuracy of its objectives and the clarity of its methods. Questions about charity work, the results achieved and the implementation of the solutions are also put forth.

The greatest impact we can have as a foundation lies in our ability to create convincing concepts and to provide models for the solutions we propose. These are the ideas which we would like to exchange during the symposium. We would like to organize an international learning forum and, at the same time, create networks for cooperation among foundations who share the same strategic orientation.

The conference here today is being held at the request of Reinhard Mohn, founder and chairman of the Bertelsmann Foundation, who demonstrates once again his decisive managerial qualities by urging us – members of the foundation community – to reflect upon the following questions: Can we learn from each other? Can we find a way to evaluate and improve the effectiveness of our projects? Is there a way of making our projects run more efficiently? What methods of cooperation do we have at our disposal for the various projects? And finally, how can we contribute to making foundation work even more effective for society?

We at the Bertelsmann Foundation, in holding this symposium, are applying one of the principles of our by-laws which states our commitment to the "research and development of innovative concepts in management and organization." We have also oriented our course towards international cooperation and understanding. We work as an internationally operating foundation in many expansive fields of activity. We deal with strategically-oriented political consulting, with training and further training courses in the media, placing the emphasis on the responsible use of the new electronic media. We examine and test methods for increasing efficiency in public administration and create models to be used for this purpose. We are committed to the reform of German higher education, for which the Center for Higher Education Development (CHE) develops concepts. The Bertelsmann Foundation seeks to establish a new basis for the social market economy and appropriate regulatory policies. It has already initiated exemplary reading encouragement projects in three model libraries. The awarding of the annual Carl Bertelsmann-Prize represents an important event in the foundation's calendar. The award for 1996 will be conferred on the most innovative school system – as always in an international comparison. Subjects of former awards have been dedicated to the areas of "Progressive Immigration and Integration Policies" (1992), "Democracy and Efficiency in Local Government" (1993), "The Social Responsibility of Televison Towards Society" (1994) and "Methods and Instruments for a Successful Employment Policy" (1995). In awarding this prize, we would like to create awareness of the most effective solution in a particular area and to learn from it, thereby providing new impetus. Special attention has been given to the international singing competition "New Voices" introduced by Liz Mohn in 1987, which promotes young talented opera and operetta singers. In all of the above-mentioned activities, we have been dedicated to our founder's convictions – *property imposes duties* – which is also a postulate of the constitution of our country.

Operating foundations as institutions of civil society

Many of our projects have elucidated the immeasurable importance that operational foundation work has on social progress. Foundations are committed solely to the duties imposed by their by-laws and by their objectives. They do not have to take into consideration the interests of any lobby nor are they obliged to take action according to a traditional set of rules imposed on them by society. They can afford to, indeed have the obligation to, raise questions which could lead to the solution of urgent social problems. They possess the potential to operate in a more flexible manner than government agencies, or than political policies or the economy. A foundation is justified in its efforts solely by the measure of success of its capacity to solve social problems. While there is no private or political party interests to which a foundation is accountable, a foundation is under the clear obligation to prove that it has utilized its privileged status to serve the real needs of the public.

Foundations meet this task when they function as institutions of the civil society. They can and must mediate between opposing interests and value systems, between differing concepts for the future. They are faced with the especially difficult task of instituting change by means of rational persuasion alone; by setting a good example and creating convincing models. There is no power base such as is held by the government or large concerns. Foundations must work by promoting their strategic suggestions, by concrete examples as to how problems could be solved; they form vital partnerships with other institutions which share their vision of a better future. The methodical process of foundation work proceeds from the definition of a problem to the discovery of solutions in concurrence with those who will be affected and the experts, to the final implementation of these solutions within the areas of society concerned. The final goal of this process is the exemplary function of the solution itself. We always hope that our model solutions develop a dynamic of their own – thus providing new impetus for others.

This quality of being a mediating, intermediary institution carries with it new challenges and tasks for foundations, however. On the one hand, foundations are able to take on new tasks within a world joined together by the global network: tasks which involve transmission and "translation" crossing cultural, social and political boundaries. On the other hand, they are faced with the difficulty of positioning their work effectively within the complex relationships of parliaments and governments, international organizations and citizens' initiatives. A certain amount of courage to act is necessary, but also the steadfastness to resist unreasonable demands. Foundations must have the capacity to see the potential of their own actions – to look "beyond their own backyard," and at the same time to see the limitations as to what can realistically be accomplished. Networking provides foundations with the opportunity to find out what is being done elsewhere – and this way of working has proven to be especially effective in the solving of extraregional problems. Networks bring together expertise and working capacity, institutes and individuals, in order to work together towards common goals from different vantage points and with varying positions of influence. Networks provide the opportunity to combine analysis and practice, paving the way for the transfer of scientific know-how to practical application.

The common search for successful methods

All of these insights have encouraged us to search during the course of this symposium for successful methods which will enable us to meet the challenges we are faced with. Among these challenges is also the question of how foundation work may achieve a more prominent place in the eyes of society. The possibilities which are available to society through foundations are often not recognized. One hopeful sign is President Herzog's decision to formulate his expectations concerning the role of foundations in society, and to share his ideas at the symposium. It is naturally also encouraging that we have found so many comrades-in-arms from all parts of the world, who through their participation want to help us to find answers to the questions posed, and to pose themselves new and better questions.

At the end of this symposium we will have a better idea of how – under what circumstances and with which methods of decision-making and evaluation – operating foundations can carry out and secure their work and goals on a long-term basis. We will obtain information about the balance of continuity and innovation which it is essential to maintain while carrying out foundation work. We will see and come to conclusions about which forms of cooperation, and which courses of action – guaranteeing the greatest chances of success – for all of our endeavors are available to us. We will be able to ascertain how the preparation for cooperative work can be improved. And we will, in the end, hopefully see how through the afore-mentioned efforts we can increase the overall effectiveness of foundation work in our society and internationally. We will have the opportunity to acknowledge and possibly to increase the importance of foundations for the innovative development of society.

At the same time we will again have to report precisely on what the chances are of using the social acceptance of foundation work as a means to attract additional funds. We will have to see whether there are strategies evolving to convince and mobilize the multitude of smaller donors so that they can contribute to ensuring that operating project work is carried out competently and successfully, and even extended. The principle of the community foundation, which has not yet been realized, could become an effective instrument for change in our own country.

Other aspects contributing to successful project work are our foundation's own internal organizational structures and degree of work efficiency. I hope that we have also been able to collect some significant ideas concerning how these organizational tasks can be mastered. Which structures within an operating foundation lead to the most effective realization of a goal aimed at influencing some aspect of society? How can we improve the competence of our employees appropriately, while maintaining the foundation's premise of flexibility? Which conclusions drawn in response to the problems of society can we apply to our own organization? How can we sustain the capacity to not become misled by short-lived trends and at the same time be able to anticipate the problems of the near future so as to be prepared and able to propose meaningful solutions in time?

Operating foundations are obliged to be innovative. They owe it to themselves and to society to set their standards high. Facing the challenges and questions of our time is the daily task of all projects of any foundation. When we step back for a moment from the daily routine and reflect upon our actions, we can see that these questions concern all aspects of foundation work. And if we do this, reflection will itself become a project.

Objectives of an operating foundation

Reinhard Mohn

In the following presentation I would like to focus on an analysis of the weak points within societal structures and to emphasize the various possibilities for operating foundations to serve as innovators in society – and the necessity of their doing so. To begin with, however, I would like to make a few personal remarks as to how I became involved in the work of foundations.

Motives for establishing the Bertelsmann Foundation

Immediately after the war I had to take on entrepreneurial responsibilities. Consequently I did not have the time nor the opportunity to pursue university studies. As a young entrepreneur I was obliged to learn a great deal very quickly. During that period I realized that the most effective way of learning was to talk to people who were doing a good job. So I always tried to get in contact with those who were the best in their fields. This method of learning ensures that nothing learned is superfluous. Most importantly, conversing with practitioners opens up opportunities for correcting mistakes and furthering self-development. This holds true not only for work in the business world but also for work in foundations. The following decades of my professional career were devoted to developing the Bertelsmann Company into a media corporation. It was a difficult period but at the same time a positive and challenging one. When an entrepreneur has learned to take charge of complex responsibilities, to organize an entire corporation and to develop solutions to problems on a daily basis, he or she will then view the structures of society, government and politics with new eyes. It becomes clear that a system of management is now reigning in these public spheres which has not been adapted to the requirements of our day.

As a result of the uneasiness I felt when I observed a society lacking order – a feeling most likely shared by all citizens and democrats – and guided by a feeling of responsibility toward the community, I felt the desire to be of assistance in improving the situation. This led – now almost twenty years ago – to the establishment of the Bertelsmann Foundation. A further motive was the wish to secure the continuity of the corporation. For many companies, the burden of inheritance taxation is too great to bear. Many of them founder because of this. Furthermore, a media corporation like Bertelsmann, dedicated to journalism and communication, is involved in a sensitive area of work which does not tolerate capital exercising too much influence well. With these considerations in mind, I transferred approximately seventy percent of the shares of the Bertelsmann Corporation to the Bertelsmann Foundation in 1993. For managerial reasons, however, the voting rights were not transferred, as the premises for corporate management differ from those necessary in the establishment and management of a foundation. For consideration of both community responsibility and corporate continuity, I thus made the decision to establish the Bertelsmann Foundation.

Deficits in our social order system

The era we live in is characterized by a change in our living conditions – on a scale and at a speed unprecedented in the cultural history of mankind. This development has been triggered by impulses resulting especially from our increased knowledge and our new technical possibilities. Under the impact of these influences we are observing the emergence of a new way in which people see themselves, which is reflected in new objectives, changing lifestyles, and higher demands and expectations. At the same time the pressure emanating from the global competition of systems inescapably confronts us with the necessity to modernize our cultural heritage. The imperfections and hardships occurring in the course of this process of transition mainly result from the inability of human beings to respond quickly enough to the changes in the underlying conditions of their lives. The basic thrust of the efforts made should be to modernize our traditional systems of order so that they meet the requirements of both the tasks and the people involved.

Peoples' cultures, their thinking patterns and their lifestyles evolved over long periods of time. Cultures reflect experiences and convictions. They are the result of numerous efforts to secure the very existence of human society. The fact that cultural development requires prolonged periods of time also helps to explain the difficulties encountered in the international process of change today.

Human beings tend to hang on to their habits – and their cultures. Cultures are based on the tried and tested. Over long periods of time it has been a dominating order principle to keep up and nurture tradition. This value put on tradition has indeed proven successful in the past as an element of order. However, the prerequisite was that relatively static living conditions prevailed and that the pillars of the social order were not called into question by external influences. Competition between different regional cultures or their integration only took place on a limited scale at the time because of the low level of mobility.

These premises for stability no longer exist in our culture today. Our world is becoming increasingly homogeneous. Cooperation, but also competition are characteristic features of our day and age. The ongoing learning process to shape a global order is proceeding under dramatic tensions. The question we therefore have to ask ourselves is whether it is possible to design this systemic change in a more efficient and humane way. At the same time we would need to examine how such a gigantic task could be coped with and what body or bodies would be suitable to take the responsibility for the updating of our order systems.

In this context an analysis of the capacity for evolution of the major order systems of our society is called for. In the following I will evaluate the areas of politics, the state, economics and cultural orientation under this aspect.

The political order

The democratic form of government is in line with the hopes and the self-perception of the people. Today's insufficient political leadership performance with the resulting dissatisfaction of the citizens has so far not been directed against the system but against the way in which it is handled. It is striking how little effort is dedicated internationally to a methodological modernization of our democratic order. The representatives of political power are obviously unable or unwilling to take the necessary initiative for a further development of the system.

The state order

The objectives, the organizational patterns and the management functions of the state, i. e. of public administration, were developed at a time when alternative performers of these functions did not exist. The most urgent objectives of the state's activities at the time were to secure equal rights for all citizens and to implement the state's rules and regulations in an orderly fashion. This concept of coping with the state's tasks turned out to be indispensable at the time and did indeed prove to be quite successful. Yet, societal conditions and requirements have changed completely in the meantime.

Both the volume and the degree of complexity of the state's tasks have multiplied. The regulatory rigidity of the state increased while its overall flexibility decreased. The urgently needed development of the objectives toward performance orientation and innovation was neglected. That those who are employed by the state have developed only a limited identification with their employer under these circumstances, is easy to understand.

The economic order

The modernization of the economic order was achieved with a relatively larger measure of success. National and global competition enforced change. Obstacles in adjusting to the changing conditions result mainly from the state failing in its regulatory policy, unions and employers pursuing misguided objectives and backward management techniques being practiced in the companies. However, these deficits are being worked on. An updating can be expected.

Values and capacity for consensus

Increased wealth, education and security have reduced the interest that people take in moral and cultural orientation. The fact that children are being brought up with a greater emphasis on individuality has only served to amplify this trend. A misguided notion of self-realization is threatening to jeopardize our moral consensus and our ability to live together as a community. The institutions that used to provide moral and cultural orientation are caught up in their own traditionalism and dogmatism. Their influence is no longer sufficient today. Their messages are, however, increasingly needed!

The above analysis of the evolutionary capacity in the areas mentioned shows serious deficits. Many of the problems we are confronted with today can be traced back to these very causes. Serious damage may be caused before the constraints of the global competition of systems force us to take action, even serious enough to endanger our social order. The question therefore emerges as in which ways and by what means we can mobilize the forces for the necessary modernization of our systems.

Strengthening competence for leadership and problem-solving

By mentioning this objective I want to point to the necessary systems development which is equally indispensable in all areas of society. Important elements of this systemic change are:

1. Making targets and performance measurable.
2. Introducing competition and performance orientation – with noticeable sanctions.
3. Decentralizing and delegating responsibility.
4. Granting freedom for thought, action and experimentation.
5. Setting targets and stipulating working conditions that people can identify with.

Any order, social or otherwise, that is designed for success and for securing its own survival must abide by these premises. Realizing these demands will cause an increase in dedication and flexibility, in creativity and innovation capacity and, above all, in human satisfaction. The non-observance of these demands will lead to stagnation and loss of competitiveness.

There remains the question why those responsible in the different fields of social activity lack the insight and the strength for innovation. Is it an excessive workload? Is it that they are too blinkered? Is it that they are afraid of change? Or is it that they truly fail to understand the situation? Perhaps it is a bit of everything. But one thing is certain: We have to move. – And we have to move fast.

The potential impulse providers

In the past science has opened up many a new avenue. Its facilities for analysis, systematic classification and research will be urgently needed in the future. The independent status of our universities offers a good basis for such innovative work. If the universities were to decide to use the success factors I mentioned before as a basis for their work, then that would be an additional bonus.

I personally see the non-profit operating foundations in very much the same starting position. A foundation can both solve individual problems and work on systems development. It is independent and only answerable to the commonweal and to its own objectives. It needs people who have learned to find answers to unresolved questions in the course of their lives. The creative people in a foundation must be committed and must also be sensitive to the self-perception of human beings. If these conditions are fulfilled, operating foundations can indeed "move mountains." Anyone who assumes the leadership of such ventures will gain many friends and lots of support.

However, the socially relevant effects of an operating foundation will only make themselves felt if and when efforts are made to secure an appropriate overall diversity. This requirement has unfortunately not yet been fulfilled in Germany – but it can be! Looking at the rate of asset formation it is reasonable to predict that we will have plenty of potential founders and committed citizens who would be willing and able to promote societal innovation. The non-profit operating foundation can become a center for such future-oriented endeavors. It seems to me to be desirable that the sponsorship of such foundations be assumed especially by companies that can make a creative conceptual contribution on the basis of their professional experience. For reasons of practicability, I personally doubt the wisdom of the call for "more entrepreneurs into politics" voiced in our country. But I do see a great opportunity of bringing entrepreneurial expertise to bear on the solution of societal problems in the context of a non-profit operating foundation. Such an approach would, at the same time, also meet the demand laid down in our constitution that "property imposes duties."

The innovation potential that a country can tap with the help of a lively community of foundations is illustrated by a comparison with the effect that the non-profit foundations have in the USA. Smaller as well as larger foundations and especially the so-called "think tanks" play an indispensable role in shaping society, especially in terms of the badly needed systemic development. The Bertelsmann Foundation puts forward the proposal that we should learn from this international experience and that we should trigger similar initiatives also in our own country. It seems to be a characteristic feature of our day and age that identical problems emerge and identical tasks have to be solved in many countries of the world. An international exchange of experience between the foundations will lead to constructive cooperation and to more rapid progress being made. In our daily lives we experience the word as a homogeneous entity. It therefore makes sense to solve the problems together.

The emphasis on the special form of the "operating foundation" here at the symposium is attributable to the mode of work adopted by the Bertelsmann Foundation. However, it needs to be pointed out at this juncture that an optimization of the overall effects of the non-profit foundations requires the existence of other forms of foundations as well. In this context I would specifically like to mention the sponsoring foundations and the non-profit institutions that examine and approve applications in the spirit of their founders. Another form of foundation which needs to be mentioned here because it is currently very successful and expanding vigorously in America is the "community foundation." This form of foundation, dedicated to the problems of a city, merits our special attention. The readiness of citizens to "do something" for their home town is surprisingly high while, at the same time, the need to take care of community services not covered by the local authorities is constantly increasing. I myself am currently in the process of creating such a "city foundation" for my home town of Gütersloh.

Out of a feeling of responsibility toward the community I established the Bertelsmann Foundation two decades ago. I was convinced that many tasks could be solved in a better way and that a failure of our systems was often at the root of many of the grievances of our time. The most serious mistakes that I discovered in the course of the work of the Bertelsmann Foundation were the unconditional defense of fiefdoms once acquired and the insistence on traditional rules in a rapidly changing world. As yet, this societal diagnosis has only partly been understood in our country. The prevailing conditions speak for themselves.

In the summer of this year I will be celebrating a very special birthday for which I wanted this symposium as a useful and valuable birthday present. In the course of my life I have learnt how important dialogue and an exchange of experience are. I therefore look forward to our exchange of views and ideas. We want to learn from you, my guests and the foundations you represent, and I am hopeful that our encounter will lead to cooperation and better understanding. Day after day all of us experience the world as one single entity. So, it makes a lot of sense to join forces and tackle the problems that it poses for us together.

In conclusion, let me thank you for attending and participating in this "Foundation Symposium". I very much hope that you will feel the richer for it after our encounter. On a personal note I would like to thank you for this wonderful birthday present. At the same time let me offer you a heartfelt vote of thanks for the food for thought and the impetus that you will be giving to foundations in this country in general and to the Bertelsmann Foundation in particular.

The responsibility of foundations

The significance of foundations in our day

President Roman Herzog

At the conference which has taken place here the last two days there was not only a theme to discuss but also an occasion to celebrate. And both were reason enough to come to Gütersloh. The subject of operating foundations has been of interest to me for a long time. As the concept of *operating foundation* has not yet been given due consideration in German terminology (and as we all know, anything which has not found expression in language cannot, according to Morgenstern, find expression in reality), it is important for me to take this opportunity to encourage the removal of this linguistic obstacle. So much for the appeal of this subject.

As I have been informed, this conference has also been secretly designated as a birthday present from the Bertelsmann Foundation to Reinhard Mohn, its founder. It is, of course, not the custom to congratulate someone before his or her birthday, and I have no intention whatsoever of doing so now. A presidential greeting could not compete with such a conference anyway. Therefore, I said to myself, "If you can't beat them, join them," and decided spontaneously to take part in the symposium.

In fact I think the best way to do justice to Reinhard Mohn, entrepreneur and philanthropist, is to reflect upon two characteristics combined in his personality: his dynamic managerial skills and his commitment to the commonweal. The tribute being paid to him and the topic of the conference are therefore entwined.

Dynamic entrepreneurial skills and service to the public are not only personal attributes worth striving for; they are, in addition, the heart of the free and democratic "civil society," the source of its vitality and precondition for its existence.

Of course, dynamic entrepreneurialism and service to the public are two distinct qualities, and in Germany they are in fact considered as separate notions. The patterns of thought which continue to prevail simply wedge the state between the two as a lever of power. The state is responsible for imposing taxation on the profits of entrepreneurial dynamics and for deciding, according to its own set of criteria, how to redistribute tax money into the public welfare system. As is becoming more and more evident, there is a risk involved that the dynamic entrepreneurial force will become crippled, the governmental machinery of redistribution too expensive and the ever-decreasing volume of money for redistribution sanded up in the already overtaxed social system.

Operating foundations are not of course the *deus ex machina* which will do away with all our problems. They illustrate, however, that things can be done differently. They are paving the way towards a merger of entrepreneurial dynamics and service to the public in a direct, spontaneous, decentralized, efficient and versatile manner.

To calculate just how much operating foundations are needed and what they are capable of, we must first have a look at the potential for development generated by the foundation landscape in our day, taking into consideration demand as well as supply. I think one can assume with confidence that the more this potential is recognized, the greater the interest will be in the entrepreneurial dynamics taking place within the process of operating foundation work.

Allow me to say a few words about the potential of foundations. First of all, they have been in existence for ages. The first known patron was Gaius Maecenas. Even in his day there was artistic talent to be promoted, social ills to be remedied and policies to be debated. Maecenas discovered Horace and Virgil and, while Octavian and Pompeius were at war in Lebanon and Egypt, he was concerned about such issues as economic development and social peace in Rome and Italy and became foreign policy adviser to the later Augustus.

The Fugger family and the Hanseatic merchants continued this tradition in the Middle Ages. Religious foundations were also important and it is hard to imagine medieval life without them.

During the Age of Enlightenment in the West, there were different attitudes towards serving the public, and these followed the various national traditions. Tocqueville described it well when he said that in France it was the state who was responsible for public welfare, in England the aristocracy, whereas in America, the people, being of a more individualistic nature, found that the concepts of citizenry, prosperity, generosity and public welfare belonged together and could not be separated.

In 19th century Germany, a mixture of Enlightenment philosophies and Judeo-Christian traditions influenced the foundation community in a way not dissimilar to the American tradition. In the period of rapid industrial expansion in Germany (around 1870), private enterprise, scientific advancement and foundation work all became an inspiration to each other. The results of this stimulus are still evident today in cities like Berlin and Frankfurt when we take a look at the museums, educational institutions and charity organizations which have remained in existence from that time.

At the time it was reaching its peak in Germany in the 20th century, this trend was violently interrupted. Two world wars, two dictatorships, enormous inflation, devastating deflation and a currency reform deprived the active citizenry of a basis for social involvement. Another result was that it took away from foundations the financial means to continue their work. The philanthropic spirit, however, never really succumbed. Such institutions as the Donor's Association for the Promotion of Sciences and Humanities in Germany, which is celebrating its 75th anniversary this year, as well as names like Krupp, Thyssen, Körber and Bosch are good examples.

A comparison with America, however, makes us painfully aware of the cultural damage our country has suffered in this century.

Based on a study by the Johns Hopkins University, the average sum donated in the U.S. amounts to DM 1200 yearly; in Germany DM 170, and in France DM 140. Americans on the average donate not less than 12 per thousand of their annual income; Germans only 3, and the French 1.5 per thousand.

One of the reasons why the donation pattern in Germany resembles more the French than the American lies in the fact that the crises which hit Europe during this century had damaging effects on both Germany and France. Another explanation, however, which is often heard nowadays, deserves reflection. The German economic post-war "miracle" and the success of the social market economy were so impressive and obvious for all to see that a rejuvenation of a highly developed foundation tradition seemed almost unnecessary. The competitiveness of the German economy appeared unassailable, the prosperity of all citizens secured, and the welfare state inexhaustible. To sum it up, the demand for foundation work was not much greater than the supply.

In the meantime we have apparently reached the limit of efficiency in both economy and state. There is talk about the capacity for technical innovation (or lack of it) in German industry. Price competitiveness is suffering due to an overvalued deutsche mark. We are being threatened to become prisoners of the successful deutsche mark. It seems that all around the world the danger of inflation has been warded off. In its place a drastic cure of debt deflation is the impending danger threatening countries with heavy debts and structural budget deficits. As a result of demographic problems and the increasing rate of unemployment, the affordability of the welfare state is now being questioned. Rising wage-related costs, rationalization resulting in a reduced number of jobs, the revaluation of the deutsche mark and the relocation of production sites of German companies abroad are turning the situation into a vicious circle. The discussion about the attractiveness of Germany as a business location is thus facing an impasse.

Taking into consideration capital assets statistics, the accumulation of private wealth in Germany has, at the same time, reached historically unique proportions. Private monetary wealth rose from 1.5 to 4 trillion DM from 1980 to 1994 alone. Resulting from an estimated 1.7 million inheritances by the year 2000, approximately 2.6 trillion DM should become available in the form of monetary and property assets. There has never been, one would like to think, such a remarkable coincidence of increased demand and growing supply in the foundation network as there is at present in Germany. There is something else which must be considered. The increases in wealth in the past decades have not been of equal benefit to all strata of the population. Wealth in western Germany is not as unevenly distributed as some maintain however. Yet it is easy to understand how this concept has come about. When the property value of condominiums, single or double family unit houses is evaluated, the cash market value is taken as a basis and not the basic site value. Considering that new social differences are, nevertheless, emerging, this may become a serious problem in the relations between East and West Germans – at the latest when the economic adjustment period is over.

In this context, foundations could also have a healing effect. For every deutsche mark and every inheritance donated to a foundation instead of to some remotely related relative, the problem could be alleviated from two sides. First, the difference in wealth between individuals would be, to a certain extent, reduced and second, the foundations on their part would assist in bridging social and regional gulfs by carrying out the work they were meant to do.

There has never been a better chance for foundations to take up the enormous challenge presented to them to become concept designers for problem-solving in our society – to become the driving force behind change.

We do not need to reject everything which has been tried and tested. But change is necessary, even if only to secure the time-tested for the future. We must equip ourselves with the necessary cultural, material and institutional provisions for the 21st century. We are talking about the future of the social community. We are talking about mutual cooperation between the sciences, the economy and society. We are talking about a new orientation of national politics in a changing world.

In my opinion, attention has been called to rewarding fields of future activity for operating foundations.

Here again we can learn from the American example. Whereas the Americans were able to continue to promote foundations uninterruptedly, the First World War brought about the beginning of the afore-mentioned cultural breach in Europe. Not so long ago, I spoke at the Stiftung Wissenschaft und Politik (SWP) Research Institute for International Affairs in Ebenhausen on the role of American think tanks and their origin in the American philosophy of pragmatism. This way of thinking, which can be felt in all spheres of public life in the United States, conceives of the relationship between theory and practice as a mutual learning process. Practice is of service to theory in that it constantly poses new questions, theory serves practice by offering alternatives. They are both a constant reminder of each other's fallibility and neither is too proud to apply the method of trial and error.

Pragmatism of this nature is something fundamentally different from an opportunistic way of reaching goals without knowledge or skill. It is a strategic problem-solving concept, a critical, rational approach to defined objectives. This seems to be, in my opinion, precisely the essence of the thesis paper which the Bertelsmann Foundation prepared for this conference on the work of operating foundations. This is exactly the characteristic which distinguishes operating foundations like the Brookings Institution, the Rand Corporation and the Bertelsmann Foundation from other types of organizations which merely provide financial backing, or from those working exclusively on program conception. The strengths of the individual types of organizations can only be brought to bear when the foundations work together in a tolerant, constructively competitive atmosphere. At the same time, these strengths will contribute to mobilizing all of the forces within the network of German foundations.

What the grantmaking foundations and the conceptual foundations have in common is that they see their task in the defining of objectives. It is up to those involved in the areas of science, business and politics to carry out these objectives. Operating foundations, on the other hand, take it upon themselves to achieve the goals they are striving for. They have to be more modest and more willing to take risks than the foundations who only set goals. They have recognized that people are not willing to accept the tendency of the social sciences to merely analyze the past or present state of affairs in a contemplative way or even to make projections about the future. The aim of operating foundations is to reflect upon the possibilities and risks of the future, to find ways to prevent the risks and ways to take advantage of the opportunities. The awareness of their fallibility compels them to continually reevaluate their strategies and chances of success and to adjust the means used to implement these strategies.

I can only warmly recommend to all those involved in the decision-making process in the economic world, society at large, in science and in politics to take up the example of this basic philosophy of operating foundations. John Dewey, one of the founders of American pragmatism, recommended to his colleagues that the only way for a philosopher (I would add here: entrepreneur, politician and patron) to look his fellowmen in the face with openness and compassion is to adopt an attitude of modesty and courage. This is indeed the method behind the work of operating foundations. I am convinced that when this method is generally adopted, our country will make a giant leap forward.

Foundations as guarantors of entrepreneurial continuity and social responsibility

Mark Wössner

There is a century-old tradition of foundation work. It all began with the medieval church foundations, which carried out fundraising activities in the manner of the Apostle Paul: "Christians should do with their possessions as if these did not belong to them at all." The more recent history of foundations, however, has been influenced by the Industrial Revolution of the 18th and 19th centuries. Over 600 foundations for the public welfare were founded in Germany alone during the course of the 19th century, including the renowned Carl Zeiss Foundation initiated by Ernst Abbe after the death of Carl Zeiss. This was the first modern foundation of its size in Germany, and it has remained till today one of the model foundations of our country. In the USA during the same period, it was successful entrepreneurs such as Andrew Carnegie and John D. Rockefeller that were engaged in public welfare work through foundations, true to the Puritan ethic connecting ownership with social responsibility.

The number of foundations in the United States is ten to twenty times greater than in Germany. This discrepancy, which works out to be 1:4 if the usual factor of comparison is applied (used in any comparison between the USA and Germany), can be explained by the heavier reliance on financing through stocks and shares of the expansion of the German economy during the years of rapid industrial expansion in Germany from 1871 onwards. Wealth was not accumulated to such an extent in families, in other words, in the hands of just a few. Two world wars, and economic and monetary crises, also help to explain this fact. Another reason for the smaller number of foundations in Germany lies in the basic difference between the German and American concepts of society. Whereas the German concept is that of the welfare state, the American social system is more clearly based upon individual responsibility.

In this decade (that is, up to the end of this century) a new generation of inheritors will take over great amounts of wealth and entrepreneurial responsibility in Germany for the first time. The third generation, following the two generations which re-built Germany after the Second World War, is now taking the stage. Large inheritances will be at its disposal. Medium-sized firms will be forced to solve the problems of finding suitable successors. Because of this fact (and due to the pressure of inheritance taxation), a wave of corporate foundations is expected in the coming years.

The main reason for this probable development towards more corporate foundations lies first of all in the efforts of the middle-class to maintain a certain continuity of its corporations. (When speaking of the middle-class, we are speaking of 60 percent of the gross national product and two-thirds of the jobs in Germany.) Continuity is to be maintained despite high inheritance taxation and other fiscal obligations, despite governmental reglementation and ever-increasing international – global – competition. These are the challenges which must be overcome.

A further reason for the increase of corporate foundations lies in the increasing sensitivity of entrepreneurs for social responsibility, which has become an integral part of their work. The famous postulate from Goethe's Faust has perhaps promted some third-generation inheritors to reflect upon their responsibilities: "That which you have inherited from your fathers – earn it – in order to possess it". There is no doubt that many families which have become the inheritors of great wealth are orienting themselves in new directions. The logical consequence of this new way of thinking and the corporate strategy of separating capital from managerial responsibility has had optimal results:

1. The quality of corporate management in firms can be maximized to a great extent by the utilization of outside expertise and the free selection of professional management.
2. The continuity of the capital can be assured simply and without inheritance taxation by the allocation of company shares without voting rights to foundations.
3. The contolling power on the capital side can still be maintained through the existence of smaller corporate shares, which carry with them certain voting rights connected with the main portion of the capital (for example the Reinhard Mohn DM 500 share).
4. The interests of the family, according to the afore-mentioned concept, are to be optimized in my opinion.

This model appears to lack any other tenable business or social alternative. However it is important, for the purpose of discussion, to pose some critical questions. Professor Dale will impressively present us with some of these concerns, for example, whether or not it is truly in the best interest of the public welfare that the owners of great wealth avoid paying the government "its due" in the form of capital and inheritance taxes. Is it socially acceptable or desirable that the obligation to pay taxes on large amounts of wealth be waived and thus money withheld from its legitimized disposition by the government? This seems to me to be an acceptable practice only if the transfer of wealth to foundations dedicated to serving the public welfare remains a limited portion of the total amount of wealth transferred in a society (that is, the transfer of wealth which is subject to inheritance taxation). Accepting this premise, the development of corporate foundations seems to me to be a very interesting contribution to the plurality of our society – and a nucleus for social innovation and evolution.

Why should successful entrepeneurs, who have proven a lifelong capacity for recognizing important trends, sound judgement, enthusiasm and creative vision, be less able to operate creatively and responsibly with funds which are virtually public than government organizations or the public administration? Reinhard Mohn is convinced that social change and rejuvenation are primarily dependent upon the presence of creative, innovative individuals. And where do these individuals come from? Are they more likely to be found in government administrative agencies or in politics than in science and industry? Why should our society have to refrain from utilizing the potential of the cooperation of private wealth with entrepeneurial creativity? Shouldn't this combination of forces be seen by society as being (potentially) beneficial?

The achievements of operating foundations in the areas of social change, in collective learning processes and in the opening up of rigid structures which have been handed down are, in my opinion, of great value today. Work done by Bertelsmann Foundation programs provides us with good examples. These include solutions to problems and suggestions for reform in the areas of education, job training and higher education, or towards more achievement-orientated leadership in local and federal government administrations; towards the unity of Europe or the redirection and restructuring of the job market; towards a cultural reorientation of society – to mention only a few of some 120 Bertelsmann projects initiated and carried out annually. All of this clearly demonstrates the capacity of foundations serving the public welfare to stimulate creative impulses and maintain social diversity.

The Bertelsmann Foundation has already spent over 300 million deutsche mark in its short history for programs such as those mentioned above. Medium-range estimates of future yearly budgets lie somewhere between 50 and 100 million deutsche mark. Long-term estimates range much higher. The wealth which has been given to the foundation by Reinhard Mohn represents 70 percent of the shares of the Bertelsmann corporation (at a value of ten billion DM, or ten billion dollars – either figure could be accurate. The sum which is being added to the Bertelsmann Foundation is vast.)

The development of the Bertelsmann Foundation was the keystone of Reinhard Mohn's concept as an entrepreneur. This incomparable conception began from the virtual wasteland of the post-war period with the development of the Bertelsmann Book Club and the mail-order business in the fifties and sixties. By this time, Mr. Mohn had already codified his own corporate "constitution." This meant that – already in the sixties – the business orientation of the corporation had been firmly established. The Bertelsmann Corporation expanded dramatically in the seventies, through the magazines of Gruner and Jahr, and through the music business and the international expansion of all activities of the corporation.

In the seventies, Reinhard Mohn engineered the present-day form of the Bertelsmann Corporation – a joint-stock company. He initiated the practice of profit-sharing for the employees, and developed along with this the financing concept of non-voting but high interest-earning dividend rights. For those who are not experts: this is something like a non-voting preference share. Mr. Mohn's concept is known today to the public as the "Bertelsmann Model."

It is a concept of partnership which attempts to balance fairly the interests of capital, employees, and management. DM 2.5 billion in profit-sharing and interest have been paid out to employees since the initiation of the profit-sharing program. Employees who have participated in this model for 25 years earn on the average a 16-month yearly salary, counting current profit-sharing and interest paid on the accumulated profit-sharing from previous years.

The central idea of this corporate concept has always been for Mr. Mohn the realization of modern management strategies; this essentially means decentralization, systematic delegation, and operational freedom for both management and individual employees.

The keystone of this corporate concept has been, again, the establishment of the foundation. While others have long since retired, Reinhard Mohn embarked on a "second" life as an entrepreneur to realize his dream of a creative, innovative operating foundation. Mr. Mohn has thus long been a leading member of the German post-war "Hall of Fame." His foundation work has put him on the list of famous German foundation endowers such as Zeiss and Bosch, and such American philanthropists as Carnegie, Rockefeller and Ford. We are proud of Reinhard Mohn's corporate concept.

Inspiring international cooperation

Ricardo Díez-Hochleitner

This most appropriate and noteworthy initiative with respect to the responsibility of foundations has been launched as part of the symposium "Operating Foundations." Although originally intended as a 75th birthday present for Reinhard Mohn, the symposium is actually a present to all of us involved in foundation work. Reinhard Mohn, one of the most formidable business leaders of our time, has demonstrated most impressively how a corporation can be made successful through partnership and ethical conduct. Moreover, he has followed his social conscience, and in establishing the Bertelsmann Foundation to which he has contributed his wealth, experience and knowledge, he continues to serve society. In creating this initiative, Reinhard Mohn is paving the way towards international cooperation among foundations based on ethics, responsibility and partnership.

In my opinion, operating foundations are the best way for private corporate initiatives to demonstrate social consciousness. The great achievements foundations have made in many countries are mainly due to the support of individual patrons and corporations. Such sponsors have always possessed an undeniable sense of social responsibility and have often been skilled in capital management. Foundations represent institutionally the best possibility for these private initiatives to give back to society part of the profits which it has legitimately earned. They thereby contribute to social progress.

We must insist on upholding and encouraging this positive trend for the future. Not only because of the social or cultural value foundations represent, but also because they ensure that private initiatives, launched in democratic states in a market economy, will in fact not be neglected. Hopefully, the days are over when the profit amassed by private enterprise is justified simply by tough competitiveness.

Transferring experience which has been gained in economic corporate management over to a form of social management not only contributes to a better image for the business, but also to a growing redistribution of income, which in turn leads to higher social returns. It is thus in the interest of nations and governments to facilitate these developments without neglecting the supervisory function they have vis à vis foundations. Foundations, on their part, should also not lose sight of the basic objectives of their founders and at the same time adapt these objectives, when necessary, to the changing conditions.

The nations of the new united Europe, which are establishing structures exactly for the purpose of achieving economic and social objectives, must become aware of the immense potential their foundations possess. Only then will these nations be in a position to overcome their current differences as to social values and principles of taxation. Foundations, on their part, have to evaluate the projects they are involved in, find out what effect they have, and work on increasing cooperation at the European and international level. This is essential if they are to fulfill their role as vanguards of social, cultural and economic progress. In this way private foundations will hold an even more eminent position in modern society.

Europe is in the process of emerging. It must therefore be consciously "designed" if it is to assist in establishing a new world order – one which is based not only on past economic and political objectives, but one which rests on an enormous cultural heritage, thus providing the potential for unlimited creativity in the arts, science and technology. This spirit, however, can only prevail if Europe adopts a culture of dialogue and cooperation. In light of the fact that this attitude can only develop out of a society of responsible and active citizens, that is to say from private initiatives, foundations could again take a leading role.

The *Zeitgeist,* however, has an influence on foundations. Their future landscape could be designed to greatly benefit modern society if the strong, presently emerging current of active citizen participation, which attempts to increase social commitment as opposed to the prevailing forces of the past, were reinforced. The source of this social current can be traced back to the increasing creativity and innovation of private management, the rapid development of new production techniques, a higher level of education and to ubiquitous mass communication, which has contributed to greater and higher social expectations.

On the other hand, seen from the perspective of the Club of Rome, we must ask ourselves: Which demands or challenges in the next few years will foundations be faced with, in which new technical developments, environmental projects and telecommunications programs will help establish a new order? How will we cope with the immigration of populations from the Third and Fourth Worlds to Europe and North America and the multicultural society it creates in its wake? What influence will fanatacism and terrorism have on the world we are living in? How will we solve the urgent problems of unemployment and in particular, youth unemployment, which represents one of the greatest concerns of all European countries and also of the rest of the world? Will foundations take it upon themselsves to support the individuals, groups and institutions who deal with these problems? Or will they prefer to take a back seat and merely resign themselves to "meaningful" and "safe" projects of a local nature? Will foundations put emphasis on the new requirements of the future? There is in any case not the shadow of a doubt that challenges and new possibilities will exist.

From everything which has been said up until now it has become clear that in some European countries a certain tendency to adjust to the new social and political rules is becoming evident. At the present time, public and private debates are taking place in some countries as to which of these private initiatives are capable of facing the urgent problems burdening European society.

We are in a period of transformation, a moment at which a private foundation can be years ahead of its time. In view of all the questions and challenges the future presents, a new foresighted concept is gaining ground in all areas of foundation work. This is due to the fact that many foundations would like to be a part of the development of the new society of the 21st century which has, in fact, already begun. This clearly proves that it is no longer important *to acquire a good image* but rather *to form and express opinions* and, thanks to research, debates and concrete experience, *to formulate* specific and global *solutions*. With these objectives in mind, foundations have to refrain from advocating a conscious political or social ideology. Their only ideology, if in fact this concept can be used at all, lies in the concern for humanity and a sense of solidarity.

This can be accomplished when the private foundation is able to demonstrate independence, competence, sympathy, integrity and most importantly objectiveness in its activities. It should not be used as an instrument in the hands of a certain lobby. As opposed to local and national governments, a foundation can bring to bear publicly, in an international context, the conclusions it has reached during its project activities. Allow me to mention the Bertelsmann Foundation in this context as one shining example of how the idea of entrepreneurial partnership with the full consciousness of a European spirit can be transferred to foundations.

Taking into consideration this new context and its urgent appeal, foundations and public administration are not adversaries and cannot be seen as such. They are, much to the contrary, complementary allies. The fact must also be recognized that at least at present public administration cannot pretend to finance the constantly growing number of creative projects society is craving. The so-called "welfare society" which has become a standard can only continue to exist as long as society is able and willing to defray the expenses it incurs. Foundations on their part will soon miss out on the chance of accomplishing the work they have been called to do if in the long term they do not strive to work together with the various administrations to secure tax benefits and to guarantee the future benefaction and continuity of their important and innovative work. Private foundations should, however, pave the way for international projects and first of all learn to listen to their potential partners. They should not lapse into a kind of cultural arrogance whereby they dictate their opinion (one inevitably connected to a certain culture) of what is best for the other society. Again, the ability to listen must be a characteristic of every foundation.

In conclusion I would also like to express my own personal conviction that the humanistic and liberal vision of society, to which private foundations have greatly contributed, still has an important objective to fulfill in order to shape the future and to assist in coping with the difficulties accompanying it. In this context, however, debates between foundations, like the ones taking place during this symposium are extremely important and necessary in inspiring international cooperation (through bilateral and multilateral projects). Such projects should be a result of the collaboration of foundations among themselves, but also, where possible, of the work done in conjunction with universities, private companies and public administration. If we hold fast to this approach and to these convictions we will have experienced the birth of the foundation of the 21st century.

The often mythical or distorted view that many people have of foundations must be modified as quickly as possible. We must start with the recognition and full support of these institutions which represent an essential part of life in a modern, democratic and foresighted nation, as well as in the European Union. I would like to conclude my presentation with the words of the Spanish author and diplomat Salvador de Madariaga that "our eyes should be idealistic and our feet realistic. We have to advance in the right direction, step by step. Our objective is to define what it is we desire, what is possible at a certain point in time within the framework of these desires. That is the way to translate these desires into possibilities."

Owing to the initiative and leadership of Mr. Mohn, the Bertelsmann Foundation has taken a giant step in the right direction by focusing our attention on the responsibilities and possibilities which an operating foundation has at its disposal to contribute to the development of international cooperation – in a spirit of solidarity and desire to spread knowledge – by laying out new paths for future society. And you, Mr. President, offer Germany a new vision and a new spirit of open dialogue and responsibility. And this feeling of responsibility will certainly come knocking on the doors of foundations. The result of this will be that not only German foundations, but all operating foundations in Europe and throughout the world will continue to provide hope for the future.

International experiences

U.S. law affecting foundations and their ownership of businesses

Harvey P. Dale

Introduction

I was asked to focus on the U.S. experience with foundations and I want to make three preliminary observations.

First, I was instructed to concentrate on the U.S. law. Because there is no good reason to suppose that any other civilized nation would want to use the U.S. law in this area as a model for its own regime, I want to make clear that these remarks should not be understood to contain any recommendation for legal action by any government. My comments are intended to help creators and operators of foundations to consider how best to structure the governance of their foundations and particularly the ownership by their foundations of business enterprises.

Second, the U.S. law is extremely technical and largely contained, for historical reasons, in our tax law, the Internal Revenue Code (I.R.C.) of 1986. I will avoid most of those technicalities and make very few references to the U.S. tax law.

Third, I will spotlight certain governance and structural issues, and the possible policy reasons affecting them. Thus, this is *not* an overview of U.S. law affecting foundations, but rather a narrow focus on a limited portion of that law – the portion dealing with foundation ownership of business enterprises. The excess business holdings rules, discussed in this outline, are not the only ones which may affect the ownership of a business by a private foundation. Several other rules, enacted in 1969, may also operate, depending upon the particular facts and circumstances.

I will first provide a brief historical overview of the U.S. situation. Second, I will discuss the policy reasons that led to the adoption of the U.S. rules. Third, I will mention a few examples of interesting private foundation structures involving business holdings. Finally, I will offer a few concluding remarks.

Brief history of the development of the relevant U.S. law

Although there were some few earlier instances of U.S. Congressional interest in private foundations, Congressional concern began to increase in 1961 when Representative Wright Patman of Texas called for hearings on possible abuses. For a decade, starting in 1962, he held hearings and issued eight installments of a report on foundations. This report was quite critical of the activities of private foundations. Among the "abuses" that he identified (abuses from his point of view) was the ownership of operating businesses by charitable foundations. Rep. Patman suggested that foundations be prevented from owning more than 3 percent of the stock of any business enterprise.

In 1965, during the process of the Patman hearings and in response to congressional requests, the U.S. Treasury Department issued a Report on Private Foundations. It, too, found reasons for concerns about private foundation ownership of businesses and recommended prohibiting private foundations from owning more than 20 percent of any unrelated business.

In February 1969 the U.S. House of Representatives began hearings on tax reform. Congress responded to the concerns expressed by Rep. Patman and the U.S. Treasury by passing the Tax Reform Act of 1969. This legislation added to the Internal Revenue Code, our tax law, an entire new chapter – about 28 pages of statutory language, later elaborated upon in over 150 pages of regulations – aimed at regulating the activities of private foundations. Among the rules adopted was one limiting the amount of stock that a private foundation could own in any business enterprise.

Ignoring a great many details these are its principal features:

1. I.R.C. § 4943 is captioned, "Taxes on Excess Business Holdings." It first imposes a 5 percent tax on the value of any such holdings and then – if the prohibited holdings are not disposed of in a timely manner – it imposes a second 200 percent tax on the value of such holdings.
2. The prohibited business holdings do not include two important exceptions:
   a. a functionally related business, which contemplates, e. g., tuition received by a university or medical fees received by a hospital, or
   b. a passive holding company deriving 95 percent of its income in the form of interest, dividends, royalties, capital gains, etc.
3. In general, a private foundation has a five-year period within which to dispose of its "excess business holdings" received by gift (that does not include excess business holdings purchased by it; those must be disposed of right away). That five-year period may be extended for an additional five years, with the consent of the Internal Revenue Service, if – despite diligent efforts to dispose of the holdings – the foundation can prove that it was impossible to sell them except at a substantially below-fair-market value.
4. "Excess business holdings" is defined to mean the ownership by a private foundation of voting stock of a business in excess of 20 percent of the total voting stock. The 20 percent threshold is reduced, however, by any voting stock owned by so-called "disqualified persons," which includes substantial contributors to the foundation and any foundation managers. Thus, for example, if a major contributor to the private foundation owns 15 percent of the voting stock of the business, the private

foundation's ownership of that business cannot exceed 5 percent. In certain instances, however, the 20 percent limit may be increased to 35 percent.
5. If "disqualified persons" do not own more than 20 percent of the voting stock, then (but only then) the foundation may hold non-voting stock of the business without limitation. Otherwise any non-voting stock is also included as "excess business holdings" and must be disposed of.
6. There are complex rules which treat "disqualified persons" as directly owning stock of the business which is in fact owned by corporations, partnerships, trusts, and other entities in which the disqualified persons have some interest.

This description, and these rules, apply only to private foundations. There are no equivalent proscriptions for public charities. The definition of a private foundation is very important and unfortunately very complex. In general, however, a private foundation is a grantmaking charity which has received its funding and assets from a small group of people rather than from the general public. Certain types of charities, e. g., schools, hospitals, and churches, are public charities and not private foundations, regardless of the source of their funding.

Policy concerns

Now, I will attempt to state the various policy concerns which have been expressed as reasons for worrying about charitable foundations owning too much of an operating business, and which gave rise to this legislation. Most of these considerations emerged during the Patman hearings, the 1965 Treasury Report, and the 1969 legislative process leading up to the enactment of the Tax Reform Act of 1969.

Each concern could be analyzed and criticized – indeed, there are quite strong reasons why some of the stated concerns are, in my view, either wrong or overstated – but my purpose here is simply to put them on the table so they can be understood. Either alone or together, and despite their weaknesses, they persuaded the U.S. Congress and President in 1969 that legislative prohibitions were desirable, and they continue to be sufficiently persuasive to prevent repeal or diminution of the sanctions enacted more than 25 years ago. I have grouped the concerns under ten headings:

1. *Deferral of charitable benefits (or giving)*
   The concern was that private foundations either might not receive adequate income from the businesses they control to enable them to sustain a vigorous grantmaking or charitable program, or that they might receive enough income but hold it rather than devoting it quickly to charitable causes. Evidence was presented suggesting that charities tended to receive less income from controlled businesses than from equivalent market portfolios.

2. *Unfair competition with for-profit businesses*
   The concern was that charities owning a business could deploy the charitable capital for business purposes as needed, while at other times holding it and investing it free of tax. For-profit businesses, not owned by charities, would either have to pay tax on the income of their own capital resources, or compete for needed capital in the capital markets.

3. *Conflicts of interest between business and charity*
   The concern was that the interests of the charitable owner might conflict with that of those running the business. For example, the charity might wish to have a high level of dividends, while the business might want to retain capital, or the business might wish to make a high-risk investment in a promising new market while the charity might prefer caution and preservation of current business values.

4. *Self-dealing*

The concern was that there are numerous ways in which people controlling the charity and the business might obtain personal benefits at the expense of the charity, e. g. use of business assets (such as office space, or even airplanes), high salaries, or valuable services, which might be viewed as too lavish by a disinterested shareholder. These suspect transactions were also viewed as being extremely difficult to police because of their frequency.

5. *Distraction of managers from charitable activities*

The concern was that the need to run an active business would consume too much time and attention of the managers of the charity, with an attendant reduction in their focus on charitable manners. I suspect that part of this notion is really something else, i. e. that the attractiveness of tax, control-perpetuating, and other benefits of private foundation ownership might tempt businessmen to create a private foundation to own their businesses when they never had any interest in charity to begin with.

6. *Erosion of tax base*

The concern was that income taxes and estate or death taxes of wealthy businessmen could be reduced or eliminated by their giving business ownership to a private foundation. That would produce a corresponding increase in the tax burden imposed on other persons and sectors of the society.

7. *Perpetuation of control*

The concern was that a private foundation could be used to maintain family control of a business for an unlimited period. This could give rise to a class of people privileged by birth, which would be at odds with the U.S. notion of a fluid society. It might also lead to management of business enterprises by people chosen by birth rather than talent, which would be at odds with the efficient functioning of the capital markets.

8. Weakening of the company's competitive ability

The concern was that placing control of a business enterprise in a private foundation improperly insulates the business and its managers from market forces. This reduction in exposure to normal capital market risks – such as those arising when a company needs access to new capital, or is subject to takeover bids – may make the enterprise less efficient and competitive, to the long-term disadvantage of its employees and the capital markets.

9. Investment portfolio policy

The concern was that having too much of the foundation's assets in the securities of a single business would adversely affect the value of and the income on its portfolio. There was some evidence that suggested that foundations tended to receive lower-than-fair-market returns on the concentrated business holdings. But even apart from evidence of lower returns, modern portfolio theory and the law of many countries teach that a fundamental duty of charitable trustees, in prudently managing their investment assets, is to diversify the portfolio to reduce or minimize uncompensated risks.

10. Unseemliness

The concern is that some people believe that it is inappropriate for charities to be running or owning commercial businesses. Some have referred to the Sermon on the Mount for the view that one should not serve both God and Mammon. Others have said "there is something unseemly about the use of a charitable organization to maintain control of a business"[1] or that "there is something fundamentally objectionable and incompatible with a foundation's effort to serve both the charity and the business interests of the donor."[2]

---

[1] John R. Labovitz, 1969 Tax Reforms Reconsidered. In: The Future of Foundations 101, 114 (1973).
[2] William H. Smith, Carolyn P. Chiechi, Private Foundations before and after the Tax Reform of 1969, 69 (1974).

Examples of private foundation structures

A. *Examples of U.S. structures*

1. The Poynter Institute was created by the will of Nelson Poynter, who died in 1978, to own the St. Petersburg Times newspaper. It also owns the Congressional Quarterly and several other medial properties. In order to avoid the excess business holding rules, the Institute persuaded the Internal Revenue Service that it qualified as an educational organization, thus avoiding private foundation status (the excess business holding rules only apply to private foundations but not public charities). The Poynter Institute carries on an extensive educational program – it has a faculty of 15 people teaching journalism and related courses. The St. Petersburg Times had revenues of about $220 million last year, and provided $4.4 million out of the total $5 million of the Institute's budget. Interestingly, if the Institute had failed to avoid the excess business holding rules, it had been forced to dispose of the newspaper which by Nelson Poynter's will would then have become property of Yale University. The affairs of the newspaper and the Institute are both managed by the same person, today Andrew Barnes, as required by the terms of the governing documents.
2. Howard Hughes Medical Institute, which used to own much of the estate of Howard Hughes, managed to qualify as a medical research institution. That made it not a private foundation thus avoiding the excess business holding rules. This not only relieved it of the obligation to dispose of concentrated holdings it received from Mr. Hughes, but also enabled it to avoid the minimum distribution rules which make private foundations in the United States distribute 5 percent of their assets each year. Its portfolio today is quite diversified and it is beginning to make substantial grants in addition to its own medical research.
3. The Kellogg Foundation receives funding from the Kellogg Foundation Trust, a wholly separate entity from the Foundation. The Trust, in turn, owns 34 percent of the Kellogg Com-

pany's common stock (down from about 47 percent in 1984, as mandated by the excess business holdings rules). The Internal Revenue Service appears to be satisfied that (in the language of the statute) effective control of the Kellogg Company lies in the hands of disinterested persons, thus allowing the trust to continue to own 34 percent (i. e., less than 35 percent) of the common stock (rather than the typical lower 20 percent) and allowing the Foundation (which does not own that stock) to continue to manage its charitable grantmaking activities without worrying about managing the Trust's portfolio. The Trust has one corporate trustee (the Bank of New York) and three individual trustees. Each of the individual trustees also serves as a director of the Foundation, and each of the individual trustees either serves or is about to serve as a director of the business, the Kellogg Company. The Kellogg Company Board of Directors has eleven members.
4. This final example from the United States, the John A. Hartford Foundation, was remarked on by Congress and has been written about substantially since then. The Hartford Foundation used to own about 20 percent of the shares of A&P, given to it in 1957 by George Hartford. The shares at one point in the 1960's were as high as $70 apiece, by in 1978 they had fallen to $5 apiece. That substantially depleted the assets of the Foundation and the shares were finally sold in 1979 to Tengelmann Warenhandelsgesellschaft.

B. Examples of structures outside the U.S.

1. The Wellcome Trust used to own control of the Wellcome Foundation company. (Note the vocabulary here: the charity is the Trust and the business is the Foundation.) The shares of the business were left to the Trust under the will of Sir Henry Wellcome. Only with the benefit of special orders from the U.K. courts was the trust able to divest itself in stages, first by selling some shares of Wellcome into the market in underwrit-

ten offerings and then (quite recently) by accepting an offer from Glaxo to dispose of its remaining 39.5 percent of the Wellcome Foundation. In the process, the income of the Trust went up dramatically. It had been less than 91 million pounds in 1991, but it was about 333 million pounds in 1995. So its medical research grants have also increased substantially. Its assets now exceed U.S. $10 billion.
2. The Nuffield Foundation used to own substantial holdings in British Leyland Motors. When the stock declined in 1975, the Foundation's assets were devastated, and its grant programs were quite significantly reduced.
3. The non-voting common stock of Barings Bank was wholly owned by (and was the principal holding of) the Barings Foundation, which was set up in 1969. After Nick Leeson worked his special magic, causing an estimated 1.4 billion pound loss to the Bank, the assets of the Baring Foundation were reduced about 85 percent, which dramatically cut the Foundation's grantmaking activities. Its grants had been about 12 million pounds in 1994. The Dutch company ING, which took over the bank's assets, agreed to underwrite the Foundation's charitable commitments for the current year, but after that Barings Foundation is on its own. The reduction in its level of giving has inflicted pain on a number of U.K. charities which had depended on funding from the Foundation.
4. The Van Leer Foundation was also set up in a tripartite fashion. The business is owned by a separate entity from the Foundation and the concentrated holdings are now in the process of being diversified with the sale of about one quarter of the holdings of the business. When that happens, the income on those assets will go up by three and a half to four times of what had been there before, allowing the foundation to increase its giving by a substantial amount.

Concluding comments

As I said, above, these policy concerns that I put forward were stated as the reasons for the legislation in the U.S. Similar if not identical concerns have been voiced in other countries. This suggests to me the desirability for a foundation – even if it is not now subject to any of such rules – to consider how to structure itself *today* so that, while meeting the goals of its founders, it will perhaps avoid *tomorrow* being "caught" or adversely affected by later-enacted legislation aimed at such perceived (even if incorrectly perceived) concerns.

I would like to suggest several governance and structural issues which private foundations with substantial business holdings might consider – I emphasize the word "consider", because my suggestions may not all be worthy and, in any event, some of them may simply be incompatible with the founders' wishes or the desired method of operation of the foundation.

1. To deal with the concern about the deferrral of charitable benefits – consider adopting some kind of spending guideline. It should not be measured by "income" (which may be constrained from time to time) but rather as a percentage of the fair fair value of the assets. It would be wise that such a guideline not be too rigid, i. e., to allow flexibility to vary the scope of charitable activities over time or in the light of unforeseen circumstances. It would be wise to provide for some method periodically to redetermine the fair market value of the foundation's assets.
2. To deal with the unfair competition concern, it might be wise to consider dealing with any concentrated business holding only on arms' length terms, and to consider generally not using charitable assets – even on arms' length terms – for the benefit of the business.
3. To deal with the conflict-of-interest concern, it might be worthwhile considering methods of locating control of the business, i. e., voting control, in an entity other than either the

business or the foundation. For example, the tripartite structure used by the Kellogg Foundation and the Van Leer Foundation might be an interesting model. The trustees or directors of such a third entity should be selected by processes designed to identify people knowledgeable about and sensitive to the needs of both the business and the foundation, and capable of balancing those needs. The tripartite concept would also address, to some extent, the concerns of distraction of managers of the foundation from their charitable activities.
4. To deal with the self-dealing concern – consider adopting a strong policy against self-dealing, and consider having it policed by periodic independent audits (perhaps by outside auditors, or perhaps by an independent audit committee).
5. To avoid the perpetuation-of-control concern two steps might be thought about:
   a. Putting in place some process for selection of future managers, of both the business and the foundation, designed to identify managers by talent. The process should both be, and – importantly – be *seen* to be, impartial and fair.
   b. Putting in place some process for possible future sale of some or all of the business holdings. Sir Henry Wellcome did not do this, a failure which cost the Wellcome Trust a lot of money, time, and trouble – because it had to go to the U.K. courts on several occasions to get the authority to dispose of its Wellcome Foundation holdings. In the fullness of time – and, because the existence of a foundation is perpetual, the relevant time frame can be quite long – there may be reasons why any given foundation will wish to, or need to, diversify or change its investments. It would be wise for founders to be involved with this question at the outset, rather than leaving it to later generations to figure out what to do without their guidance. This process would also help address the investment portfolio diversification concern.

Operating foundations in Europe

Rüdiger Stephan

Any discussion of foundations in Europe means taking into consideration their proverbial diversity and many-sidedness. There is hardly a better reflection of Europe – of its history and culture – than can be found in its foundations; no description is able to completely capture the wide variety of foundations that exist. During this symposium we are discussing operating foundations, which are without a doubt the most important form of foundation with respect to social commitment and responsibility. Our field of vision has thus been narrowed considerably. There are approximately 2000 operating foundations – about five percent of all foundations – in the United States. The European Foundation Center has estimated that there are about 8000 operating foundations in Europe, which represents ten percent of all foundations. I would, however, judge this number to be somewhat too high.

The focus of this symposium upon operating foundations legitimates the emphasis of my paper upon the work of the European Cultural Foundation and the international cooperation of foundations. I will cite practical examples of foundation work in order to discuss those questions relating to the assessment of the need for active social involvement and international cooperation.

The work of the European Cultural Foundation

The work of the foundation, with which I have been associated for a year, has been very broadly defined: it is to support activities and research related to culture and education which have a multinational dimension and are Europe-orientated. This open approach has meant that the foundation has been able to initiate and in some cases carry out programs which you may recognize, for example the "Erasmus," "Tempus," or "Eurydice" programs. In addition to this, European institutes for the environment, for education, and for the media have been created.

On the one hand, this open definition of the foundation's work encourages creative enterprise in general, those engaged in cultural and socially-oriented activities, and the willingness on the part of individuals to make commitments and to take risks. On the other hand, such openness forces the foundation to continually review priorities and projects in the light of ongoing changing conditions, in order to ensure that the foundation continues to fulfill its obligations to society successfully. This "voluntary obligation" to review priorities and projects led, in addition to the instigation of thematically-bound projects, to the initiation of a first geo-political priority for Central and Eastern Europe in 1987, and to a second prioritization of the Mediterranean region in 1993.

The work of the European Cultural Foundation is guided by the following basic questions:

1. What are the greatest challenges and problems facing Europe at the present time? An adequate answer to this question could be provided by referring to the catalogue of questions dealt with by European institutions such as the Council of Europe or the European Commission. However, the recognition of the realities of daily life takes us into homes and to the working place. While continuing to maintain and support cultural diversity, we see our task in the development of a European civil society living together in peace, freedom and security.
2. The foundation must deal with the question of the contribution of cultural phenomena to the overcoming of the great chal-

lenges and the solving of our current problems. I would like to illustrate the importance of this question with the following example: The relationship between the European and the Islamic worlds is in need of a constructive in-depth dialogue. The question of the contribution of cultural phenomena with respect to this dialogue extends beyond cultural or scientific exchanges per se. It touches upon political and economic spheres, even upon matters such as domestic and foreign security.
3. What lies within the practicable possibilities of the European Cultural Foundation? In view of the many tasks connected, for example, with the development of a Central and Eastern European civil society, those tasks taken on by the foundation must be clearly defined.

The free competition of ideas should not become crippling rivalry. It is much more important to give top priority to long-term effort-encouraging and effort-unifying involvement. Projects of the European Cultural Foundation, such as the project supporting the exchange of experiences concerning democratic processes and decision-making in various areas of society by parliamentarians of different nations, or another project supporting the discussion of democracy and freedom in Central and Eastern European cultural magazines, in short the support of intellectual and cultural inter-relationships, can only be of lasting effect and thus be of value if they are planned on a long-term basis and carefully developed into the future.

Learning from criticism

The results of a recently published study state that fifty American and European foundations have spent 411 million dollars since 1989 to support the democratization process – to develop the concept of active citizenry – in central Europe. The Soros Foundation heads the list. Although the efforts of the foundations on the whole have been good, there have been sobering and often disap-

pointing results in recent years. The study states that this has happened:
- when the necessity of longer-termed involvement (not only of a financial nature) was not recognized,
- when the foundations involved did not operate inter-actively – that is, they not only developed their own problem-solving strategy, but also carried this strategy out without involving or cooperating with local organizations,
- when foundations neglected to pursue the potentialities of working together with private and public agencies, or with other foundations.

It is also interesting to note that two areas have been neglected by foundations up to now: the areas of education and the media.

The European Cultural Foundation is also confronting another question: What can it do for the development of the "house of Europe"? Should not other foundations, besides the Bertelsmann Foundation, also be asking themselves this question? The European Commission appears to have realized that foundations have the potential to influence the development of a concept of European civil society. The Commission has thus been keen to exchange ideas with foundations, and foundations, on their part, should be developing ideas in this direction.

Forging links in cooperation with other institutions

In order to develop relations beyond the Mediterranean with the regions of the Near East, North Africa and Europe, between the Islamic and the European worlds, links must be forged, not only between the societies in the nations of the continent of Europe, but also between the Islamic-influenced nations of the southern and eastern Mediterranean regions. It may be comparatively easy to establish a forum for European-Islamic discussions, presupposing that there is a willingness to communicate. The problem lies in finding common ground upon which these differing cultures can come together and communicate with one another. The topic of our discussions for 1996 is "cosmopolitanism." It will be interesting to see whether this topic provides a common ground for real understanding – beyond the level of discussion in the sense of merely exchanging ideas.

In addition to this, we see it as one of our important tasks to develop "preventative therapies" for fighting mutual ignorance within the European and Islamic worlds. Knowledge of one another should not be limited to sensational news stories or the reports of war correspondants. One example of this "therapeutic" concept is the "Mémoires de la Méditerranée," a series of publications – autobiographies, historical accounts of daily life in Arabic societies – which have been published simultaneously in various European languages. The project was made possible by a flexible agreement between publishing companies, experts in the field, and the European Cultural Foundation. Forms of organization such as this form a positive basis for cooperative work. The same applies to the plan to initiate a parallel program – if possible together with other foundations – which would present information and knowledge about Europe to the Arabic nations.

Allow me to mention yet another example of international cooperation, in this case cooperation between public and private institutions. Some of you may be familiar with the legendary School of Toledo, the medieval center of Christian, Judaic and Islamic culture and science, the influence of which was felt particularly in northern Europe. Toledo is experiencing a Renaissance today, thanks to the cooperative efforts and support of local and regional agencies and the European Cultural Foundation.

The cooperation which is taking place in the initial planning stages of programs may be even more successful. American and European foundations, including the European Cultural Foundation, have initiated the so-called "Balkan Commission," which will present its report mid-year, containing suggestions and recommendations to governments, international organizations, and public and private agencies concerning long-term peace-keeping solutions for this age-old battlefield on the southern flank of Europe. The ideas presented to this crossroads of the Orient and Occident are attempts to overcome the threat of war and hatred, and are contributions to the process of establishing free democratic societies.

The precursors of this project are to be found as far back as the First World War. The foundations involved are well aware of the fact that there is a high risk in the funding of this program – something which is regarded as taboo, particularly by German foundations. As a matter of fact, if no nation or community of nations has been able to succeed in establishing a lasting peace in this region of clashing ethnic groups, cultures and religions, it may seem more than justifiable to regard the project with scepticism. Isn't a private (foundation) initiative somewhat naive?

However, wasn't there a friendship treaty signed between the archenemies Germany and France just seventeen years after the end of World War II – a time period no longer than a childhood? This was made possible because individuals and private organizations began to work towards a reconciliation immediately after the end of the war. They did not wait for their governments to negotiate treaties. They laid the foundations for the actual treaty, which then represented not the beginning, but rather a milestone on the way to the partnership between Germany and France.

There are similarities here to another treaty – the "good-neighbor" treaty between Germany and Poland, signed in 1990. Well before this treaty was signed, the "wall" between the two nations had been eroding away due to decades of efforts at mutual understanding and reconciliation which took place inofficially, below the governmental level. Looking back at the Iron Curtain and the conventions of war, it could be claimed that an operating foundation such as the Robert Bosch Foundation was involved in subversive activities. Yet despite the burdens of the past, and considering all the problems of understanding – particularly in the border areas – German-Polish cooperation is progressing rapidly because of the commitment of individual mediators and their organizations in the past; looking back over two hundred years of history, an almost incredible development.

There are negative examples as well. We need only to look at the difficulties which exist, despite a few individual efforts, in the relations between Germany and the Netherlands, and to an even greater extent, between Germany and the Czech Republic. The importance and influence of international non-governmental co-operation – which is in a wider sense cultural – is also taken seriously by precisely the anti-democratic, repressive powers which are being fought against. This is clearly demonstrated by Belgrade's recent ban of the Soros Foundation.

The importance of the international perspective

Does all of this mean that a form of private international politics or private foreign affairs is being practiced? In view of the role of government-level foreign policy, this question must obviously be dismissed, not only because of the different level of operation and means employed. International operating foundations develop visions and initiate activities which are in many ways comparable to those of business corporations. They do not primarily represent national interests, but rather, "individual" concerns with various topics, fields, and problem areas. Thus the primary goal is not the achieving of specific interests, but rather a project-oriented consensus of interests and the joining together of efforts and means in the areas of education and culture, in the sciences and in social fields.

Operating foundation work cannot be effective in achieving social change without adopting an international perspective. The truism that foreign policy is always, (and ever-increasingly so in today's world) to a certain extent domestic policy – and vice versa – applies here. Cultural, educational and social efforts often entail international multicultural elements. The so-called third sector is defined by its extension beyond borders, its "transnationality" – not only because of the new European dimension which is being promoted by the European Union, the European institutions and the Council of Europe, but also because of the very nature of the challenges and tasks which can no longer be seen nor dealt with within the specific boundaries of nations.

Taking into consideration the growing dimensions and ever-increasing complexity of the challenges our society is faced with, it seems clear that the role and importance of the third sector – particularly that of the foundations – is coming more and more to the fore. The foundations' capacity for international cooperation is thus crucial. The prerequisite for successful international cooperation on the part of foundations is a sound knowledge of their respective partners and a precise definition of the common program or project goals, and a careful coordination of ongoing evaluation and of public relations work. In addition to the multiplication of mental and material resources, the advantages of such cooperation lie in the wider scope of influence – also in geographical terms – and in the greater depth of influence possible. Reliable partners can bring their local and regional reputation to bear, and can contribute their knowledge of the specific social and cultural traits of an area, essential for the development of any project. Partnerships with Polish or Hungarian foundations in the development of projects in Central or Eastern Europe, for example, or joint efforts with Spanish or Portuguese foundations for projects in the Mediterranean region, can almost guarantee good chances of success for programs focusing on these regions.

It is not only the content and goals of any given project which, if successful, contribute to the improvement of international relations. The act of carrying out a project is in itself a vehicle for promoting international cooperation. Both partners become involved in learning processes and gain experiences which can only further the practice of international cooperation. The following example serves to illustrate this point. The positive experiences gained from the establishment of a Polish children and youth foundation in Warsaw, which was initiated by the American International Children and Youth Foundation in cooperation with a German foundation partner, and this constructive partnership itself, subsequently formed the basis for the establishment of a German children and youth foundation in eastern Germany. This was accomplished through the cooperative efforts of both public and private agencies.

The far-reaching changes of our times, as we near the end of the twentieth century, make new forms of solidarity and cooperation in government and in society essential – and increasingly so on an international level. The involvement and commitment of citizens and the institutions created by them to serve the public welfare should be recognized, and the role of these institutions in the overcoming of problems and conflicts given its due.

With ownership comes responsibility, and the same applies to property which has been entrusted to one by others; this becomes even more of a guideline when acting in the interests of the public. There is no institution which is better able to fulfill this obligation and take on today's challenges in society than an operating foundation. A serious consideration of the role of such foundations, of the expansion and improvement of their work, and of the prerequisites for such work is an investment in the future of our society and in the future of Europe.

Japan's experiences with operating foundations

Mikio Kato

Large numbers but diminutive assets and giving

Let me begin with a quick overview of the state of the foundation community in Japan with some basic statistics, though I am fully aware that statistics do not necessarily reveal the true reality. According to a comprehensive survey report released last year by the Sasakawa Peace Foundation, in Japan there exist as many as 20000 organizations which can be classified either as a foundation or an association in the loosest sense of each word, all serving a wide spectrum of public interests, ranging from education, health, foreign aid, the environment, human rights, culture, sports and recreation to policy research.

Of these 20000 so-called foundations or associations with legal status (this figure excludes all those numerous small organizations which do not enjoy this legal status), only 5 percent date back to the pre-war period. About one fourth were established with the approval of the national government, while the rest came into being with the approval of local government (i. e., prefectural governments). However, it is impossible to single out operating foundations because many of them are playing mixed functions: grantmaking, award-giving, managing of public facilities such as concert halls, art museums and sports arenas, funding research projects, organizing international conferences and cultural events, etc. It is safe, however, to say that there are very, very few, if any, operating foundations which satisfy all the characterizations made in the theses of this symposium[1], particularly the one that an operating foundation "generates, tests, and implements innovative strategies for solving societal problems it takes up." In any event, the total annual spending in the non-profit sector embracing these 20000 organizations, according to the survey report, amounted to 8.3 trillion yen or $18 billion dollars in 1988, which accounts for about 2.7 percent of Japan's GNP for that year.

The foundation community of 20000 actors of all kinds provides 200000 jobs which account for 0.4 percent of the total national employment. These figures alone are indeed quite impressive, and one may be tempted to regard Japan as an advanced country in terms of the development of the third sector or "independent sector," as John W. Gardner prefers to call it. A closer scrutiny beneath the surface of these statistics, however, soon reveals a picture quite different from the one the statistics may suggest.

What stands out quickly is the diminutiveness or smallness of assets, revenues and spending of Japanese foundations. For example, the number of foundations whose annual spending exceeds one million U.S. dollars is less than 5 percent. This diminutiveness becomes distinctive, particularly when compared to American foundations. There is no big foundation in Japan comparable to the Ford, Rockefeller, Paul Getty, or W. Kellogg foundations. Of course, we cannot and should not judge the work of foundations from the sheer size of spending alone, because what counts most is the quality of its social impact. Nevertheless, the size of spending is certainly one of the barometers to measure foundation work. Considering the enormous accumulation of wealth during the past two decades or so in Japan, one cannot help wondering why big foundations have yet to emerge.

---

1 Cf. annex, p. 155.

The subordination of the third sector to government and business

A more serious weakness of Japanese foundation operations, which may be a result of, or at least related to, the financial diminutiveness, is a peculiar relation between the first sector (i. e., the national or prefectural government), and the third sector, with the latter being strongly subordinate to the former. There are several reasons for this and they are also closely interrelated.

One is the heavy reliance of the first sector on government funding. Another is the fact that the establishment of foundations themselves was often initiated by the government sector for the purpose of meeting a particular public need on the assumption that it could be better met through an entity separated, at least organizationally, from the government, but kept under its close supervision and control. According to Akira Iriyama, president of the Sasakawa Peace Foundation, at least half of the 20000 foundations or associations in Japan are functioning under the total or very close control of government agents of various kinds.

Furthermore, these foundations are governed and managed by *amakudari* officials. *Amakudari* is a Japanese expression referring to retired government officials "descending from the heaven" of high government offices to the private sector. These former government officials are in general more inclined to the maintenance of the status quo than to testing new ideas and taking risks in implementing them. This kind of attitude of foundation directors hinders the healthy development of much-needed professionalism and of the accumulation of expertise and know-how in running foundations, let alone the constant renewal of sense of mission and enthusiasm. Even in the case of more independent and private foundations such as corporate foundations, a similar practice of *amakudari*, retired or soon-to-retire corporate directors descending to the corporate foundation to run it, can be commonly observed.

The notorious iron triangle among government, bureaucrats and business in Japan, which has often blocked any rapid and drastic change in the Japanese system, seems to have so deeply and extensively penetrated into the third sector that many Japanese foundations have become mere subsidiaries or agents of the government or the second sector, and they are unable to play one of the most critical roles of being an actor of the third sector, to "generate, test and implement innovative strategies for societal problems."

This deplorable state has its roots deep in the historical and socio-cultural development of Japan, whose successful process of modernization since the mid-19th century required a highly centralized power structure and dominant role of the central government. To catch up with advanced industrial nations of the West had long been not only the single most important national purpose but also the national aspiration without dispute. To attain this national goal, the centralization of power and a strong government with an extensive network of hierarchical ties down to the grassroots level proved most effective in mobilizing national efforts. The Confucian values which had long been the underpinnings of the moral and the behavioral patterns of the Japanese people – being inducive to a strong propensity to accept authority and thereby readily showing a high level of respect and trust toward those who hold the power – also reinforced the development of the efficiency and achievement-oriented Japanese system. Hence, a willing corporation between the government and the governed rather than an adversary relationship (like in the U.S.) has been the rule, not the exception.

This relationship remained little changed, or I should say was rather reinforced throughout most of the post-war period until recently, and it may partly account for the miraculous rapid recovery of the Japanese war-devastated economy and the eventual emergence of Japan as an economic superpower today. Indeed, as long as the national purposes are clear and there exists popular consensus as to how to achieve them, there seems little or no need or room for the third sector to play a role.

This successful Japanese system therefore has retarded the healthy development of the third sector, which is one of the crucial components of any democratic society. Furthermore, it nurtured an over-confidence in the government sector that they are not only wise enough and capable enough to identify all the public needs but also to meet them most efficiently and effectively, thus consigning the lot of people to the role of mere taxpayers. "Japan Inc." had felt little need for a serious third sector. During the mid 1970's and 1980's many corporate foundations emerged, but the basic concept they pronounced was not to serve as a vehicle to "generate, test and implement" new ideas and alternatives, but to serve within the framework of the existing system, and corporate foundations were in general regarded as an expression of gratitude for the prosperity of companies.

Another weakness of Japanese foundations is their highly ritualized structure of governance and of the decision-making process. For example, the absence of any institutionalized mechanism for self-renewing the composition of the Board of Directors or Trustees is commonly observed, and one can easily imagine where this will lead to. Human nature tends to work more towards the preservation of the status quo, which is often fortified by multiple layers of vested interests, than towards changing the status quo, and it is never easy to innovate the existing system, particularly so, if the system has been successful. We often fail to discern the sign of inevitable change and sometimes deliberately turn a deaf ear to the steadily approaching sound of the footsteps of the future.

The emergence of a new vital third sector

Thus far, I have only painted a very dark picture of Japan's third sector, and so to do justice to it, I should turn to the brighter and the more encouraging signs of changes as well.

Having accomplished Japan's century-old national aspiration to catch up with the Western industrial powers through a single-minded pursuit of economic nationalism during the post-war period, the national purpose has quickly become obscure, while a new one is yet to be found. The old values which sustained and strengthened the unified national struggle to attain these national objectives have also been gradually eroded. Material affluence accompanied by an increase disposable income and leisure hours, an erosion of the old work ethic, the massive entry of women and foreign workers into the Japanese labor market, urbanization, an increase of the nuclear family, a growing awareness of environmental depletion, the rise of a consumer movement, intensified criticism from abroad against "Japan Inc.", all these and many other factors have combined into a strong undercurrent to drive Japan toward a more individualistic and multi-value society in which the traditional relation between the first sector and third sector has also begun to change.

During the late 1970's and 1980's new foundations and associations mushroomed in Japan, reflecting economic affluence, regained self-confidence, and – more significantly – increased awareness of the limited capacity of the government sector to meet highly diversified public interests and of the rising need for small but flexible voluntary organizations capable of tapping grassroots energies. The activities of these newly emerged non-governmental organizations (NGOs) or non-profit organizations (NPOs) covered almost all areas of public concern, ranging from being the watch-dog for foreign aid, supporting foreign students, workers and refugees, guarding health services for the elderly, gender equality, protection of the environment and you name it. Interestingly enough, many of them were initiated and run by young people and are highly action-oriented. In contrast to the large foundations and associations, whose headquarters are mostly located in big urban centers, these small organizations with no legal status, let alone tax benefits, are spread all over the nation including even remote rural communities. Indeed, the Japanese people seem to have begun to practise the universal belief that a civil society is a society in which individuals have the right not only to speak out but also to organize themselves for the pursuit of a common human interest as they perceive it.

The phenomenal increase of small but action-oriented NGOs or

NPOs has led to the establishment of such organizations as the Japanese NGO Center for International Coorporation (1987); the Foundation Library Center of Japan (1988); the Council for Better Corporate Citizenship (1989); and the Association for Corporate Support for the Arts (1990), all of which are private and intended to facilitate communication, coordination and interaction not only among themselves but also with their counterparts outside Japan.

This new trend was followed in 1990 by a significant liberalization of the laws related to tax-deductible contributions. The liberalized laws extended the category of Japanese non-profit organizations entitled to receive tax-deductible contributions. As a result, approximately 1000 Japanese foundations or NPOs are now able to enjoy this privilege, though the government still tightly retains the power to determine which particular non-profit organizations are to be granted this status (which is subject to strict review every two years).

Another encouraging change took place in 1991. The Ministry of Posts and Telecommunication, which also functions as the administrator of the enormous amount of postal savings in Japan, introduced a very interesting and new system by which 20 percent of the interest earned by depositors will be distributed, with the prior consent of depositors, to Japanese NGOs working in the area of international cooperation and assistance. The total distributed last year amounted to approximately $24 million dollars.

Drastic change, however, had to wait until early 1995. In Japanese history dramatic changes often have required overwhelming *gaiatsu* or pressure from outside, particularly from foreign countries, rather than creative energies generated and pent up within. The beginning of dramatic change in the passive and reactive state of the Japanese actors in the third sector was no exception. But in this case it was not foreign pressure but a devastating force of nature. In the early morning of January 17, 1995, Kobe and its vicinity was hit by a Richter scale 7.5 earthquake, which together with subsequent fires reduced the area to ashes and debris, killing more than 6000 people and making millions of people homeless overnight.

This catastrophe of unprecedented scale revealed the inadequacy or incompetence of the bureaucratized, cumbersome, routinized and slow-moving government sector to cope with the crisis. Most significantly, it also revealed, to the surprise of many Japanese themselves, the tremendous energies of voluntarism in Japan. While the government sector failed to take quick rescue and relief actions, voluntary groups of all kinds and from all parts of Japan and elsewhere, including foreign countries, rushed to the disaster-stricken scene on foot or by whatever means of transportation available either to rescue the victims or to take specific actions to reduce in every imaginable way their agonies and sufferings. Without the brave and spontaneous actions of these voluntary groups the physical and human damage brought about by the earthquake would have been much greater.

The Kobe earthquake has indeed been the catalyst for the release of long dammed-up springwaters of volunteerism and humanitarianism in Japan, the lack of which has long been a target of foreign criticism and even accusation. The remarkable work done by such numerous small voluntary groups galvanized the whole nation with admiration and a realization of the crucial roles they could play. Now volunteerism, philanthropy, NGOs and NPOs are quickly becoming household words in Japan. Furthermore, both the ruling coalition parties and the major opposition party are competing with each other in drafting new legislation which will remove as much as possible the bureaucratic barriers blocking small voluntary groups from organizing themselves into legitimate actors in Japanese society with legal status and tax-exempt benefits. It may be safe to predict the passage of a bill by the National Diet in the near future. I am very pleased to close my presentation by bringing these good tidings from Japan.

Reports from the workshops

Workshop I
Governance and strategy of foundations
Moderation: Joel L. Fleishman

The first part of this workshop focussed on the role of foundations in society. The discussion was started by an introduction of Dr. James D. Hunter, Professor of Sociology and Religious Studies at the University of Virginia in Charlottesville and author of two books that caused a lot of debates in the U.S.: *Culture Wars* and *Before the shooting begins. Searching for democracy in America's culture wars.*

Hunter began by presenting his analysis of the unique nature of this moment in time at the end of the 20th century. He is of the opinion that the animating impulses and legitimating ideals of the Western world are now in a process of disintegration, and the nature of pluralism itself tends to provide corrosive effects. The result of this disintegration is political fragmentation and polarization; competing moral visions have (in the case of the U.S.) led to "culture wars," i. e. normative conflicts over questions like abortion, values in school, race relations. According to Hunter, public discourse is increasingly reduced to a shouting match, and democratic ideals like justice, freedom and tolerance are at risk of becoming empty clichés. He believes that state and public institutions suffer from a legitimation crisis because what is legitimate concerning social policy and innovation for one side is completely illegitimate for another group. Normative conflicts, according to Hunter, precede violent conflicts, thus "culture wars" often precede shooting wars. While the phenomena he described are most evident in the U.S. he sees evidence for them in other countries, too.

The basic question for Hunter is: How do the institutions of civil society relate to this context? He considers the institutions of higher education and philanthropy as the most important institutions in this context because of their independence, their flexibility, and the kind of innovation they are known for. Philanthropy in particular is referred to as an agent of change and an institution that challenges the existing order. However, Hunter is of the opinion that in the U.S. philanthropy often aggravates conflict rather than mediating it by funding one side of the cultural conflict. He thinks that the elites of foundations, as in most institutions of civil society (like churches, universities), exist on extremes and are fairly isolated from the people they represent.

Hunter's introduction triggered a lively debate in the workshop. Several people criticized his analysis as being too negative and argued that he ignored the fact that it has been a huge cultural achievement to liberate many people from political and social bondage. Contrary to Hunter, for quite a few speakers the fact that foundations support a variety of individual interests is one of their major assets because the healthy competition between these interests will eventually create a new concept of society. Interestingly, most of Hunter's critics in the workshop were from Germany where, as Count Strachwitz, executive director of Maecenata Management GmbH, put it, individual creativity has been blocked by a concept of society based on the model of a pyramid with every single aspect of society being forced to fit into this pyramid at a pregiven stage. Someone else added that the worst thing to tell foundations was to back off particular concerns in the interest of avoiding conflict. However, there were also supporters (from the U.S.) of Hunter's analysis of the role of foundations in the "culture wars." Robert B. Goldmann, in charge of European issues at the Anti-Defamation-League, New York, expressed the view that foundations often had not carefully considered the foreseeable consequences of their activities and had not paid enough attention to the complaints and concerns articulated by many people.

Although everybody in the discussion agreed that philanthropic institutions could have a crucial part in rebuilding social trust, and in acting as agents of change, no consensus was achieved as to the question of whether foundations should act as "neutral" intermediary agencies harmonizing conflicts or as institutions that take up and support specific interests.

The clarification process on the term "operating foundation" that followed brought more clarity to the question of the specific potential of foundations. In the U.S. the term operating foundation has a special legal meaning: It describes a foundation that is confined to running its own program inhouse (usually institutions that run museums, hospitals, etc.). The concept of operating foundations used at the Bertelsmann Foundation conference is a different one: strategic program initiating as opposed to reactive, "trendy" grantmaking. As most of the significant U.S. grantmaking foundations also base their grantmaking on strategic thinking, workshop moderator Joel Fleishman suggested to underplay the reference to operating foundations in talking about the work of the Bertelsmann Foundation in the future as it aims to be strategic not only in the procedural sense and how it goes about formulating its program but also in the substance of its grantmaking: strategic in building models of social institutional change that society might choose to implement broadly.

One participant reminded those present of the fact that compared to the institutions of the state and to the size of the world's economic product, foundations are small. Therefore they can only achieve something if they understand the concept of leverage, i. e. philanthropy has to discover niches where it can accomplish something and find partners to work with. For this reason foundations should not only provide suggestions but turn suggestions into models that will be adopted by others.

Following this argument, the participants in the workshop agreed that foundations use their potential in the best way when, after analyzing problems, they develop solutions and build models which capture public interest and gain the support of political and government officials. The "model-constructing role" of foundations should be preferred to the "criticism-of-government and social-institutions role" as criticism without credible, workable alternative models tends to engender hostility, and this indeed can create fragmentation and polarization in society.

The second part of the workshop focussed on governance issues, i. e. on the question of how foundations, particularly foundations that are closely related to a large company, can structure themselves for the future so as to continue to assure their freedom and their capacity to serve society, to be a critic of government and other social institutions, and to adapt to the changing circumstances of the future. The basic context of the discussion in the workshop had been provided by Harvey P. Dale's statement (in the plenary session) of the policy concerns that led to extensive legislation in the U.S. regarding private foundations and ownership issues.

The discussion in the workshop was opened by Rolf Möller, former Secretary General of the Volkswagen Foundation, and Count Strachwitz, with their accounts of governance issues with respect to European foundations. Möller gave a brief overview of the history of the Volkswagen Foundation and its governance structure. Although the foundation bears a name which could lead to the assumption that it is an institution created by the Volkswagen company, this is not true. After World War II the corporation was in need of new ownership as it used to be owned by Nazi organizations which had gone out of existence. The Volkswagen Foundation was created by a contract between the Federal Republic of Germany and the federal state of Lower Saxony. Its assets are derived from the proceeds made by selling the shares of the corporation. The Federal Republic and Lower Saxony each took 20 percent of the shares and passed the rights to earn profits from these to the Foundation, too. The Volkswagen Foundation was not created to act as owner of the Corporation, and therefore it is not indebted to the Volkswagen Corporation in any way.

Möller explained that he personally was not supportive of the idea of creating foundations in order to guarantee the continuity of corporations as the responsibilities of running a business and managing a foundation were both highly demanding but very different functions. According to Möller, another problem was that for a foundation which depends on the fluctuating income derived from company shares, it could be difficult to be a reliable partner to grantees and to follow (as in the case of operating foundations) long-term strategies. A third concern was that the return on assets would be smaller if the foundation was the owner of a company.

The governance structure of the Volkswagen Foundation is based on various underlying principles that allow the foundation, according to Möller, great flexibility in realizing its mission and in inviting a variety of perspectives and opinions. Among these principles is a rotation system of *Kuratorium* (board of trustees) members and the requirement that decisions of the board need a two-thirds majority. The rotation system practically leads to a built-in process reflection concerning the foundation's priorities. The board members are appointed by the founders, i. e. one half by the federal and another by the Lower Saxonian government. The mission of the foundation to provide support for research and the teaching of sciences and technology was worded in such a way that the Kuratorium was to be responsible for all details of translating the mission into grantmaking.

Count Strachwitz provided an overview of the legal and societal context in which foundations in Germany and in most of Europe operate. He explained that it was not so much the financial aspects the mission of the foundation or its governance that described a foundation but rather the technical legal framework. In Germany this legal framework has developed over many centuries. The oldest German foundation still in existence is over 1000 years old. Many modern aspects of foundations in the late 20th century (like the relationship between a foundation and a business corporation) do not describe the full legality and meaning of what a foundation is. The very old traditional foundations were formed by citizens individually and almost exclusively for health and social purposes (to operate hospitals and aid organizations). Then gradually other causes developed like promotion of the arts, humanities, sciences, etc. Still today, a foundation in Germany is judged very much by what it actually does: Does it support what it was created to support? To this day it is the founder(s) who determine what a foundation must do for all "eternity". The scope of change of the founder's original intention is still very narrow. Therefore, the scope laid down in the statutes should indeed be as wide as possible to allow future boards to adapt.

As to the question concerning a foundation's source of income, there is a major difference between the situation in the U.S. as Dale sees it and that of Germany when there are fewer restrictions. There are quite a number of foundations that are 100 percent owners of business corporations; a number are partowners of business corporations, a lot of foundations have investments in real estate or other activities, in agricultural or forestry production units, and some of course have an ordinary portfolio. As to foundations connected with business corporations there are two very distinct types: a) foundations that own to a large extent a business corporation (e. g. Bosch Foundation), and b) foundations set up by corporations for communication purposes (e. g. Deutsche Bank Cultural Foundation). The latter are much smaller in scale, usually have a small endowment and receive the funds from the corporation, however, they are not owners (let alone substantial owners) of the corporation.

Some foundations in Germany do not derive their income from an endowment at all, but rely on donations, government money or on fees for their services. A foundation that operates a hospital has no endowment except for the building as such; its income is derived exclusively from what the social security system and private patients pay for the treatment in the hospital.

The basis of the German system is that the assets are free from regulation. However, there is a limit to the foundation's activities in financial terms. A foundation is not allowed to become an entrepreneur itself if it is to retain its charitable status. Charitable status does not come automatically to a foundation (this is a separate set of regulations) although about 96 percent of German foundations do have charitable status. If they operate any kind of business activity, this must be separated in the books and in management. This occasionally presents difficulties when a small foundation tries to have the same person as managing director of the company that it is connected to and of the foundation as well. This does not work as it leads to the assumption that the foundation has become a business enterprise. The reason why one of the old and famous foundations in Germany, the Carl-Zeiss-Foundation, cannot obtain charitable status is because the corporation and the foundation are not legally separated. While a foundation that does have a charitable status pays no taxes whatsoever (neither income, property, nor inheritance tax), a foundation without this status which carries on business activities, must be taxed in the same way as any other business corporation. In the case of Zeiss, all foundation donations are subject to taxation.

All foundations in Germany are supervised by the government in two ways: by the Internal Revenue Service in the same way as other legal entities, and by a special government agency that is in charge of the activities of foundations. Foundation legislation and supervision fall into the realm of the federal states. Supervision only relates to the fact that the foundation acts according to the law of the land and according to its own statutes. It is not the government's business to know to whom a foundation gives a grant, though the authorities do check whether the foundation makes grants for the specific purposes stated in its mission. However, there have been cases of government agencies trying to interfere inappropriately with the activities of a foundation.

After the reports of Möller and Count Strachwitz, a number of participants (foundation founders, board members and professionals) outlined several features of the governance structure of their foundation. This overview pointed to the fact that foundation structures may take quite diverse forms. According to the views expressed, this should be considered an asset as foundations have a specific role to perform in society – the role of individualism. Their variety and diversity make them different from the standardized methods government uses in its work, and they contribute positively to developing a society which is able to utilize many different methods of work.

Then, the discussion focussed on several aspects of the relationship between a foundation and the corporation it is connected to. The major points of debate were the below-market rate of returns that foundations which own business corporations may get on their assets (as several examples show), and the structuring of the governing bodies. Count Strachwitz pointed out that in Germany foundations were not expected to try to gain the maximum revenue possible. Their major goal was to preserve their assets in perpetuity.

The workshop participants agreed that the more important foundations get, the more significant the discussions will become concerning their power and the potential abuse of it. This may lead to new legislation affecting foundations in Europe, too. In such a situation the most important thing is to be able to show that a foundation has carefully considered the risks and potential abuse of power and that it has tried to put in place appropriate processes to deal with them. Should it, for example, become relevant for the Bertelsmann Foundation one day to sell its shares of the Bertelsmann Corp., it should be able to make clear that this was contemplated at the beginning and that an appropriate and feasible process was put in place.

The workshop came to an end with the remarks of Karl Ludwig Schweisfurth, the founder of the Schweisfurth Foundation, Munich, who described in a very moving way how he created a foundation by means of the assets he accumulated as an entrepreneur. Full of enthusiasm, he talked about the excitement, pleasure and pride he derived from having established a foundation and he mentioned a question he often asks himself: "How can I make plausible to the many other people in Germany and all over the world (who have a lot of money and who do not know what do to with it) how much pleasure it gives you and what a wonderful feeling it is to contribute something to a worthy cause. It makes you feel that you can actually achieve something."

Workshop II
Cooperation of foundations
Moderation: Wolfgang H. Reinicke

One conclusion that must be drawn from the workshop is that much more work is required in order to achieve a better understanding of what exactly foundations have in mind and attempt to do when they talk about cooperation. For example, at the beginning of the workshop participants noted that there was not even a clear definition of cooperation. One useful suggestion was to draw a distinction between cooperation and collaboration, the latter of which should be considered a much more in-depth form of cooperation. In addition, participants noted that there was such a vast variety of foundations (e. g. issue-oriented versus a more general orientation, operational versus pure grantmaking foundations, differences in size, etc.) that it seemed difficult if not misleading to attempt to develop some general principles and recommendations about cooperation, various degrees of collaboration, or even institutionalized partnerships among foundations. Each individual case is likely to be very specific and should be treated as such. Foundations can cooperate at a number of different levels as well as in various functional areas. In order to facilitate the discussion in the workshop, the issues were divided into a micro- and macro-sphere or levels of cooperative/collaborative issues.

There was a general consensus in the workshop that foundations do not differ very much from the world of politics and the world of economics as far as cooperation is concerned and thus in many ways it remains a rather difficult if not elusive goal. Of course everybody wants to cooperate and signals such an intent. Cooperation or even strategic partnership has become a big buzzword in the foundation world, just as it is in the corporate world and the world of international politics. At the same time, however, potential partners quickly realize how very difficult cooperation is, once they start negotiating the exact structure of a cooperative venture and the exact nature of their common interests.

Why is that the case? Why is it so difficult for foundations to cooperate? One participant put it to the point by noting that one of the major hurdles to cooperation was "the pride of initiative". Every foundation wants to enjoy the pride and recognition of being the initiator of a project. In many ways foundations are sponsors; often they are sponsors of the public interest, sponsors of public goods. As a sponsor, of course, you do want to be recognized. However, given the nature of foundation work, there are very few tangible returns that can be shared and clearly and fairly divided up. It follows that it is very difficult to establish clear lines of authority and divisions of rights, responsibilities and rewards when you do cooperate.

When foundations start to explore cooperation, they should ensure sufficient transparency and disclosure from the beginning. It is prudent to let each side participate in the early stages of formulating a cooperative project. However, once two or more foundations have agreed that there is some common interest and that this common interest can be translated into a joint project, it subsequently makes a lot of sense to develop a clear division of labor, i. e. to assign the rights and responsibilities of each partner very clearly and early on. All issues related to the management of a project should either primarily be in the hands of one single partner or be subject to the "home country rule," i. e. wherever the activity takes place, the local partner is responsible. In general, though, it does not make much sense to divide the managerial responsibilities among various foundations because this could lead to a lot of duplication, cutting across different countries and creating considerable inefficiency. In any case, it makes sense to agree early on as to a clear division of labor: how the project will be run, what the output will be, and how that output will be presented.

The loosest form of cooperation among foundations is to exchange and share information. Here the topic "Internet" was brought up and the question as to what degree this emerging network for global communication could facilitate the exchange of project information among foundations. Many foundations have established their own home page but there is as yet no single common electronic space where potential projects could be discussed. Of course, the pride of initiative issue does play a role here but that should not deter foundations from exploring other possibilities for future partnerships. Cooperation would also be useful (and would not involve any major commitment) if foundations would join forces in becoming "cheerleaders" in order to find out if there were common interests that they would like to be put on the agenda of governments, or to be thrown into public debate. By joining forces they could get other foundations interested and motivated to provide resources and thus have a sort of mobilizing effect. This is especially the case for the rising number of transnational issues that should be on the agenda of foundations.

Cooperation should also be seen as an effort to avoid duplication. One interesting aspect in trying to facilitate this form of loose cooperation is the notion and concept of "affinity groups" which exist in the U.S. and in Germany. In the U.S. this practice is being facilitated by the Council on Foundations, in Germany by the Bundesverband Deutscher Stiftungen. Affinity groups get together on a functional or issue-oriented basis because they are interested in similar issues. There is no formal commitment, they simply sit down together and exchange ideas and information on a particular area, such as environmental protection, health care issues, human rights, internal violence, ethnic conflict, security issues, economic issues, etc. This is a loose form of cooperation that turned out to be quite successful in the cases of both Germany and the U.S.

More recently a number of organizations have been created for the purpose of establishing networks of foundations on a regional level. The Asia Pacific Philanthropy Consortium has members from Japan, Korea, Thailand, Hong Kong, the Philippines, and Australia. It has started to initiate cooperation on a regional level by establishing a common database. In the future, the consortium plans to organize more in-depth exchange among foundations in that part of the world. Similarly, the European Foundation Centre in Brussels (with 140 member foundations from various countries in Europe) has taken up a variety of responsibilities, among them organizing an exchange of information on a European level, generating foundation projects across national borders, developing a code of practice for foundations valid in all European countries, and acting as a united force in legal matters regarding foundations.

Switching over to more in-depth forms of cooperation, the workshop participants actually decided to call such agreements "collaboration" because they truly involve a greater commitment, often a long term commitment, and could even develop into a partnership. Here the easiest and most straight-forward type is financing a finite, limited project such as a workshop, a conference, a publication or any combination thereof. There is some commitment but a limited one. A second form would be collaboration on a more long-term basis. A foundation interested in a particular issue starts with a project as well as a commitment for a number of years without having yet laid out the exact nature of the cooperative structure that it is trying to establish. At the same time, it is obvious for the foundation that the issue is so important that it can only be resolved on a larger scale (either cross-regional or even international). This can take various forms. A number of foundations can agree to start the project jointly, or a single foundation may want to allocate in advance a certain amount of funds to demonstrate its commitment and start the project. It might then expand and broaden the project by seeking partners for cooperation as the project evolves, since the nature of the issues might change such that cooperation is vital for success. Finally, a much deeper form of collaboration would be not only to collaborate financially but also to actually establish jointly the structures, institutions and mechanisms which help to resolve a particular issue of concern. Thus, foundations would actually become involved in building the institutional network or infrastructure that deals with the particular problem, e. g. environmental protection, education, democratic governance, etc.

A number of additional factors were identified that were thought to be of relevance, depending on how deeply a foundation wants to get involved. Many participants argued that since the workshop agreed on the notion of different degrees of cooperation, it would make a lot of sense to start off with a set of relatively modest goals, i. e. with a simple cooperative project, and not to make any great commitment. As in other areas of international interaction, there is a learning curve present. In addition, foundations have to establish trust among each other as well as a reputation of reliability. It is important to understand the different cultural, legal, and often political environments that foundations have to operate in to be successful in their own natural surroundings. It should not come as a surprise that these national variations could well lead to differences during the implementation process. Subsequently, over the years foundations may well be more willing to enlarge their commitment if the early phase of cooperation was successful. So why not start off small and see whether you have common interests and ideas, similar practices and styles of management? Or if there are differences, agree that they do not in any way inhibit success. In this way, foundations can develop over the years a close working relationship and would be willing to engage in deeper cooperation and make greater commitments.

In addition, three other issues were identified that were considered important if foundations want to learn to cooperate. First of all, it should be made quite clear which type of cooperation is sought, i. e. what exactly it is you want to cooperate on; not just some broad areas (like ethnic conflict, health care, education, environmental cooperation, etc.), but the specific area of health care, ethnic violence or education. You may even want to talk about the kinds of solutions that you have in mind: Which form of environmental protection are you particularly interested in? Or do you want to do a comparative analysis? Do you just want to enhance public awareness or are you interested in promoting market-based incentive instruments to solve environmental problems? What exactly is it that each partner is interested in and is there sufficient overlap?

Second, the issue has to be truly important. In many of the topics that were identified for successful cooperation, a sense of crisis and urgency brought people together and allowed them to overcome the initial hurdles that are involved in any cooperative engagement. If the sense of crisis, as in the case of the former Yugoslavia or the Aids epidemic, is so considerable, it may move foundations to get together and to do something even though they may differ on certain operational aspects. If you were thinking about a cooperative project for the sheer sake of cooperation (because you are interested in learning to cooperate), you may want to pick an issue that is clearly perceived in different countries as central and of great importance.

Finally, if you collaborate, i. e. if you make some financial commitment, at least initially it may make sense to ensure that there is a high probability of success within a limited and reasonable time period, so that after a year or two you can actually point to something that is the product of the cooperative process. You may not need that later on, but again – if you think about deepening your relationship as you go along – it may be a clear indicator that allows you to evaluate whether you are successful in cooperating or not.

There may be yet another way to make cooperation essential to the success of the effort: to bring together two foundations with different comparative advantages. One example given was a foundation that had geographic expertise in a particular region or country, while another foundation had the functional expertise on a particular issue area. Together they went to that region and cooperated on that specific functional issue. In this particular case it was the International Youth Foundation together with the Bosch Foundation that set up a foundation for children and young adults in Poland. The Bosch Foundation had the geographic expertise in Poland, while the Youth Foundation had the functional expertise of dealing with children. Together they generated great synergy effects and due to each other's comparative advantage there were no turf fights and competition was minimal. This may be an interesting way to approach the issue of cooperation.

Foundations represent a certain social group in society, sometimes identified as the third sector, vis-à-vis the public sector and the private sector. Another way of finding ideas for cooperation and getting to know each other would be to discuss common interests in the larger society; i. e. to share and exchange ideas and information about your country's respective tax laws as far as philanthropy is concerned and how to lobby governments to change those laws, or how to make foundations more attractive and well-known. In other words, cooperation among foundations can also be highly useful to strengthen the position of foundations in their respective societies.

Yet another form of cooperation focusses on foundations as initiators of cooperation between the third sector and the other sectors of society. What about cooperation between foundations and the public sector, in particular international organizations such as the World Bank and the United Nations and the broad array of its agencies where the role of NGOs has grown considerably? What about cooperation between foundations and the private sector? Here the private sector participants indicated that for them it would be extremely helpful to be able to access information on the Internet; they could log in and find out what foundations were doing, especially in industrializing countries where the whole notion of foundations is not well developed. These countries would like to engage in philanthropy but do not know how. Is there any way for them to tap an information network where they can find out what is available and what they can do in a particular region in order to help?

Switching to the macro-level, the most important theme that came up in the workshop was the topic of globalization. Societies, not just economies, are becoming more global, and therefore foundations also have to become more regionally and globally-oriented, a task for which the regional cooperative organizations in Asia and Europe mentioned above are well placed. However, in order to better examine any future role of foundations it is first of all necessary to get a better understanding of the concept of globalization. More specifically, before foundations start to think about how globalization affects them, they must have an understanding of what it means and then see whether or not it affects their work.

From the perspective of foundations, the most important aspect as far as globalization is concerned is for them to consider themselves as providers of public goods, as organizations which act in the public interest or which at least help to enlarge the market for social and public goods. So far, globalization has been primarily an industry-level phenomenon. It is a corporate strategy. Therefore, in many ways there is an increasing mismatch between the organizational structures of private interests and those of public interest; i. e. the geography of private interests is becoming increasingly global but also more detached from territorially-based concepts like the nation state, where public goods for the most part have been and continue to be provided. Here is where foundations come into play. The fact that the private sector is thinking increasingly in global terms creates a major problem for foundations as in many ways their thinking and acting remains confined to the territorially-fixed concept of the nation state. However, as providers of public or social goods, they need to think globally as well, if economic processes become increasingly global. Incidentally, this does not mean that they cannot continue to take action locally, especially when they cooperate with a number of partners responsible for a broad geographic area.

Here two issues come into play: The more the economic dimension of society becomes globalized, the greater is the possibility of a clash between differing national ideas on what is and is not in the public interest and on how public goods are provided, i. e. how policy is made. Thus, we must compare the ways in which nations provide public goods. Here the goal is to create a learning community among foundations: What can they learn from each other as providers of public goods? To what degree can the experience in other countries be used and implanted in one's own country? Much care has to be applied in making such comparisons because one cannot simply take one system and impose it on another. Still, it certainly would be a fruitful area of collaboration. There is a second, probably even more important dimension to this. If it is true that private interests (and markets where those interests interact) are operating more and more on a global scale, then it is only natural to assume that the external frame-work and the public welfare issue brought about by any market economy will increasingly be generated on a global scale, too. This raises the question of whether foundations should increasingly collaborate in order to provide certain public goods on a global scale and to act in some areas in the global public interest. In other words, the globalization of economic processes is likely to call for a globalization of those mechanisms which deal not only with its positive but also its negative consequences.

However, as societies become progressively global and subsequently attempt to provide public goods on an international basis the old top-heavy, highly centralized instruments of governance as we know them from the nation state-based polity can no longer do them justice. In other words, it is certain that we will not have a global government. As a result, foundations could well be asked to take on a much more in-depth role in the provision of public goods; that is, not just in initiating debates, probing issues and tugging at the sleeves of politicians. Rather, governments facing an increasingly complex, technology-driven and thus more dynamic and constantly changing societal environment may well find it useful to "outsource" certain aspects of the public policymaking process to different and, more importantly, better suited social actors: foundations, the private sector, international organizations, and others. In such a scenario, foundations would be challenged to take on actual responsibilities in the public policymaking process wherever and whenever they are best equipped and positioned to do so. That of course implies that foundations would become part of a global, often functionally but not territorially-based policy network parallel to the emerging global economy. Participants agreed that this was certainly a new and innovative way of thinking about the future role of foundations – one which can no longer go unnoticed.

However, if foundations do take on greater responsibility in providing public goods, then a number of issues will arise that need to be addressed early on. For example, there is the question of authority, legitimacy, and even democracy. Governments are democratically elected institutions. The electoral process allows citizens to re-evaluate policymakers at regular intervals. Who gives foundations the authority and legitimacy to act in the public interest? How can one measure the performance of foundations if they take on such an important role?

There is also the important question of continuity. If certain important functions of the public policymaking process are outsourced to foundations, who will guarantee that the foundations remain interested in this particular issue? How can continuity be guaranteed? These and other issues require much more reflection. Foundations have to approach these issues with a certain degree of humility. Their funds are limited and there is only so much they can do. Even if foundations take on much more responsibility at the global level, they have to see their own limitations from a political perspective, as well as in terms of authority and financing. Thus, what foundations could primarily do is provide seed money, put pressure on governments – even at the international level – and initiate processes. Perhaps in certain areas where they have a comparative advantage vis-à-vis government, the private sector, other non-governmental organizations and international organizations, and they could find a niche and provide their specific expertise. Hence despite all the talk about globalization, the role of foundations as social actors will remain limited, it can and will become even more important if foundations succeed in pooling their resources, sharing their expertise and joining forces to shape the public debate and its outcome.

Workshop III
Effectiveness and legitimacy of foundations

Moderation: Rien van Gendt

Effectiveness and legitimacy are both quite complex issues, and they are interconnected. Foundations have to deal with them every day. A problem is that, as a rule, foundations operate in an environment where there are large constituencies with conflicting expectations. Luc Tayart de Borms, deputy secretary general of the King Baudouin Foundation in Brussels, took the example of this foundation to show how much creativity a foundation needs to employ in order to establish its legitimacy towards a variety of different groups.

Various aspects of legitimacy were discussed in the workshops. First of all, legitimacy is often embodied in the vision of the founder with the board members serving as trustees in preserving the legacy of the founder. Normally that vision has been translated into the statutes of a foundation. Derived from the statutes it has a mandate, a statement of its mission and concrete objectives. In other words, the intention of the founder has been translated into practical terms.

Dr. Michael Zöller, professor of sociology at the University of Bayreuth, stated in his introduction that especially in the U.S., the legitimacy of foundations and their political role in society had been subject to extensive controversy. Among the most-discussed issues is the "immortality" of foundations. Populist distrust is not (like in Europe) primarily directed against politicians but just as much against foundation managers. There is a fear that because missions of foundations are often formulated in a rather open way foundation managers would be allowed to do whatever they wanted once the founder was no longer involved in the foundation.

The debate in the U.S. points to the fact that the legitimacy of a foundation also depends on what it contributes to society. It is a moral obligation for foundations not to be driven by self-interest but by a commitment to the commonwealth. Their tax-exempt status implies their responsibility to society and their accountability. If there is too much dependence on the vision of the founder, it could detract from the relevance of a foundation and increase its vulnerability. The founder and the vision of the founder are just one element in a dynamic process where adjustments have to be made to the new realities of the environment in which a foundation functions. It is therefore important to look at issues like operating style, organizational structure, mobility of staff, partnerships, renewal of the board and contacts with the media.

A second issue related to legitimacy is that foundations are sometimes accused of being elitist by the outside world because it is not clear on whose behalf they speak. In this respect they are considered to be different from governments that are democratically elected. Foundations should counter this way of thinking and be self-confident in what they do. Foundations are in a different position from governments; they have a different legitimacy. Politicians try to implement the result of political consensus or majority thinking. In contrast to this, foundations can test and challenge such a consensus. They do not have to represent the majority, and they do not have to follow the mainstream; they can be unpredictable. Independent thinking, social entrepreneurship, bringing in social venture capital and "playing the wild card" are important for a foundation to become the engine for development. This does not always mean an exclusive commitment to innovation. There are times when foundations may have to act as preservers of values and attitudes in society.

The third issue regarding legitimacy discussed in the workshop was whether foundations should fill the gap of failing governments, i. e. should they perform functions politicians fail to perform? The answer is that foundations cannot become main service providers. They should not let governments "off the hook", particularly when under the label of enhancing civil society, government responsibility is actually being withdrawn because of budget constraints. Foundations are not a substitute for governments, they can only be complementary.

As a fourth point of dealing with legitimacy, developments were observed by workshop participants whereby foundations (often in partnership with other foundations with similar value-systems) became involved in the applied social sciences in a way which affected their operations and made them labelled by some of their opponents as "philanthropically correct." They end up losing their independence, becoming partisan and the instrument of interest groups.

Last point on the legitimacy issue: There was a discussion in the workshop on the need for self-regulation and for a code of practice. In some countries associations or foundations are working on such a code of practice. The European Foundation Centre just adopted a code of practice, and in the U.S. the Council on Foundations already agreed on such rules quite some time ago. The purpose of a code of practice is to counteract misconceptions and prejudices about foundations in the public mind and to bind foundations to certain standards. It is important that the sector itself takes the initiative in formulating such a code of conduct and in acting upon self-imposed rules instead of waiting until a ministry of finance or the European Parliament will intervene. Once it exists, it will also facilitate partnerships with other foundations adhering to the same code of conduct.

Recently, in the Netherlands a report on foundations was published in the press which stated that these were accumulating wealth without doing any grantmaking and without delivering any financial account to the general public. Also, there are foundations related to corporations that are used for commercial purposes. These illustrations show that a code of practice can be quite useful. A foundation that has a mandate but no operational program and that accumulates wealth acts to the detriment of tax revenues and does not have a basis for existence. Therefore, besides the significance, implementation and management of an operational program, ist is crucial that the mandate be realized through innovative strategies and clearly defined instruments. Apart from that, it is necessary to measure the achievement of objectives through concrete, output-oriented activities and accountability. In this sense, legitimacy is closely connected to effectiveness, even though effectiveness is a different concept than efficiency. While efficiency is more related to input with the good management of financial and human resources, effectiveness relates more to the output side.

The following ten points concerning effectiveness were presented by moderator Rien van Gendt. While all of them were endorsed by the workshop participants, some were discussed in more depth, and a few others were added.

1. The importance of a clear mandate
A foundation's clear mandate has considerable influence on its effectiveness. Resources should not be scattered but have a sharp focus.

2. Foundations as learning organizations
Particularly for grantmaking foundations it is necessary not just to make grants but to learn from the grant holders from field-based projects. Thus, a learning loop is created in the sense that lessons learned through practice are not only communicated to the outside world but are also fed back to the foundation itself to enhance the effectiveness of future grantmaking. So, foundations should become learning organizations.

3. Systematic long-term approaches
Foundations should not be driven by gut feelings. They should not be do-gooders, nor should they create short-term illusions. Foundations should try to achieve a lasting impact on the basis of systematic data-collection and problem-solving. That implies taking a long-haul approach and avoiding quick fixes.

4. Accountability and transparency

Accountability and transparency should go beyond the board of trustees of a foundation in order to acknowledge that foundations have a wider responsibility to society and to the general public. They are tax-exempt and that puts an obligation on them. It implies that they are transparent and should publish annual accounts.

5. Evaluation

Foundations need to have their projects and activities evaluated, enabling them to take a look at the long-term effects. Evaluation deals with projects, but should also deal with the foundation itself, and with its governance. Are trustees indeed involved in the governance or rather in the management of a foundation? How does the board of trustees renew itself? Are they primarily interested in input, in new proposals coming in and thus in becoming a voting platform for grantmaking proposals, or are they interested in the effectiveness of finished activities? Evaluation implies a learning dimension, both for the individuals in a foundation and for the organization as such.

The subject of evaluation was discussed in detail in the workshop. It was agreed that evaluation could only be carried out if there were at least some quantitative or qualitative benchmarks and concrete targets a foundation was striving to achieve. However, there is a danger that foundations, in order to be able to evaluate, start doing things simply because the results can be measured. Also, the participants agreed that there were projects which were difficult to evaluate, e. g. when it comes to supporting the modern arts or music projects.

Another point concerning evaluation is the importance of goal-free evaluation. It should not necessarily focus on the question of whether originally stated objectives have been achieved as these can change during the process. There needs to be a wider impact scope for evaluation.

The Bertelsmann Foundation recently developed an evaluation manual. The internal process of shaping the rules turned out to be a major learning process in itself because it showed how important it is to not only specify goals and the whole process of implementation in a very precise way but also to clearly define criteria for evaluation. Although the Foundation has done evaluation before, the intense process of developing the manual has made the evaluation process much more systematized and efficient.

One participant expressed the view that while the Bertelsmann Foundation could be congratulated for its thorough evaluation methods, most foundations did not have the financial resources to engage in comprehensive evaluation processes.

6. *Output orientation*

An output orientation is another important point in order to be effective. This has consequences for many foundations in either looking at incoming proposals or, in the case of operating foundations, for their internal projects. Less attention should be paid to lengthy need statements and descriptions of activities, whereas more attention should be paid to the goals to be achieved and to questions like: What do we want to achieve? What is the likelihood that we will be able to do it? This will also have consequences for the budgeting of such activities where single items are becoming less important than the attention paid to the presentation of budgets related to specific performance targets.

7. *Experimentation*

Accountability is important but it should not prevent a foundation from taking risks. There should be a scope for the unconventional, and therefore foundations (more so than governments) are in the position to give social venture capital, thereby contributing to the generation of new ideas.

8. *Permission to make mistakes*

Foundations should be allowed to make mistakes as long as the errors can be used to improve performance.

9. Building partnerships
Partnerships with other foundations are an instrument for effectiveness. They are crucial not just for co-funding but also for co-thinking, for increased accountability and for sometimes taking a wholistic approach as the mandates of other foundations may be complementary to your own. However, the word partnership also applies to the organization receiving a foundation's grants. A professional foundation does not make a donation but has a negotiated contract with an organization; therefore, partnerships mean a joint commitment to success, shared agendas, readiness to admit problems, to grant flexibility and mutual trust, but also to hold a critical dialog.

10. Innovative approaches leading to systemic change
A foundation should not be satisfied with a successful experiment in an incubator if the step to systemic change cannot be made. There is nothing valuable about a nice innovative approach if it stays that nice innovative approach and if the transition from a project to a system cannot be made.

A participant added two more points to the list:

11. Getting the message across
When a foundation really wants to effect change in society, it is not only important to have the right ideas, to find suitable partners and to implement a good project. From the beginning of a project, it is crucial to pay attention to the question whether and how the project and the suggested solutions can be conveyed to the general public. In fact, the communication of a project should be considered as part of its implementation. Also, the public relations work of a foundation should be – like all other aspects of its work – subject to evaluation.

12. Addressing specific target groups
In a society characterized by fragmentation it is necessary for a foundation to weigh which groups it is going to address and via

which groups it will communicate its projects. For example, if a foundation aims at making the work of the Institutions of the European Community more efficient, it is not sufficient to publish a study or to bring experts together to talk. The foundation also has to take into consideration the channels of communication and the specific target groups via which it wants to get its findings across.

One important channel of communication for foundations is the Internet. Several foundations have started to use it by setting up homepages. Communication via the Internet is not a way to target specific groups; it is communication into an unspecified universe. Thus, it is still a matter of exploring and testing how foundations can use the possibilities the Internet offers. Moderator Rien van Gendt concluded by describing a cartoon he saw a few days ago: "A manager is jumping onto a train, most probably a foundation manager. It is a train in motion and on the train it says 'Internet'. The man says: 'Well, I don't know, where it is going to, but I certainly cannot afford to miss it'."

Workshop IV
Efficiency and management of foundations
Moderation: Craig Kennedy

The discussion in this workshop focussed on how foundations can deploy their financial and human resources most efficiently. Efficiency was defined by Lloyd N. Morrisett, president of the Markle Foundation in New York, as a relationship between resources and result, or as a relationship between some measure of input and some measure of output. It is of great importance what measures of result are chosen and how inputs are measured. An important secondary question in the workshop was how foundations can remain vital and dynamic even as they grow older and the staff and trustees have developed more concrete ideas about what should be done.

It is obvious that foundations are very unique institutions. They are not exposed to the kinds of external pressures to be efficient the way that corporations are or – some would even argue – the way government bureaucracies are. The managers of foundations do not have to answer to bankers or to shareholders nor do they have to answer to the voters. It is also true that their activities are often so unique and so different from one another that comparing cost and efficiency among them is very difficult.

Finally, the goals and objectives of foundations often are not subject to simple measures of efficiency. Just as it is difficult to talk about efficiency in the context of foundations, another line of discussion in the workshop was the danger of overemphasizing efficiency so that it creates a negative environment in which foundations no longer do what they do best: encourage innovation and risk-taking institutions. These concerns often cause foundations to carry out their projects as cheaply as possible. In fact, creating false economies in the name of efficiency is probably a greater sin in the foundation community than spending too much money on a project or institution.

With that context in mind, the workshop participants grappled with the question: Which structures and methods will encourage efficient management of the financial and human resources of a foundation while still maintaining its ability to be innovative and risk-taking? Seven clusters of ideas came up during the discussion:

1. Quality of the trustees
Everyone agreed that a core issue in having a foundation that uses its resources most effectively is the quality of the trustees and their involvement in actually monitoring the work of the foundation. When there are inefficiencies, it is often because foundation directors are not being as attentive and watchful as they should be. Although almost everyone in the room was a foundation staff member and it was therefore quite easy to blame trustees and directors for the inefficiencies of foundations, this did not play down the point that good management practices really have to start at the top of the organization with the trustees. A crucial challenge is the renewal of a foundation's board and keeping it dynamic and really believing in the mission of the foundation.

2. Performance-oriented leadership
There has to be real leadership on the issue of efficiency from the chief executive of the institution. Performance-oriented leadership has to go beyond getting projects done on time. It means creating an environment of trust where issues of effectiveness and efficiency can be discussed openly. Several people in the workshop referred to creating a learning environment where people feel that it is safe to talk about their failures as well as their successes.

3. Clear goals, priorities, and objectives
There is a need for very well-defined goals, priorities, and objectives for foundation projects. One issue was that, in any foundation project, there will be different aspects which may be subject to evaluation, assessment, or monitoring at any given time. Many of the projects undertaken by foundations are very long-term efforts. This implies that in the short term you cannot necessarily assess the effectiveness of a project as a whole but you can look at certain aspects. So it is necessary to have very clear goals and objectives set for the short-term evaluations and assessments.

4. Selection of projects
Another issue of major significance is how to select projects that are going to ensure that a foundation makes good use of its resources without becoming so conservative that it avoids innovation and risk-taking. Foundations have to take risks but they have to do so with a very disciplined, systematic approach.

Lloyd Morrisett introduced a very important framework in the workshop. He talked about four kinds of risk that foundations face:

a) "Financial risk" relates to the determination of how much money a foundation should invest in a certain idea. It may risk undercapitalization because it is putting too little money into a project, given the size of the issue. Conversely, it may put too much money in a highly speculative project.

b) "Organizational risk" refers to the capacity of an organization or a group to undertake a project. The question is whether the grantee is capable of carrying out the task. Foundations ordinarily try to minimize the organizational risk by examining the organization it works with in order to see if it has a good track record, and whether its administration is controlled properly.

c) "People risk" implies that the specific people involved might not have the skills or competences to undertake the project even if the organization a foundation is working with may be an effective one. Foundations try to minimize people risk by making judgments about whether there is really the talent to get the job done.

d) "Idea risk" points to the question of whether there are indications that an idea can take hold although other people or organizations will not finance it because they fear it may not work.

Werner Weidenfeld added another factor: timing. Often foundations have a very good project but they undertake it at the wrong time which means that they spend a lot of money on an effort that really was before its time and then perhaps will be put on a shelf. Thus, the research is wasted because the foundation did not think carefully about timing.

In talking about how to evaluate these risks people in the workshop pointed out that some of the risks like the organization and people risk could be assessed very early and very carefully in the evaluation process. Others like the idea risk or even timing were more difficult and required bringing other resources, other expertise from outside of the institution, to bear.

5. Ongoing evaluation

There needs to be an ongoing evaluation of projects and activities within the foundation. One-time assessments after having completed a project are not enough; there has to be a sense that every project is evaluated, thought about, assessed every day through dialog between staff and supervisors and through the use of various other mechanisms. Again, there is a strong emphasis on the internal culture of an institution that allows people to talk carefully and openly about their failures as well as their successes. However, for many institutions it is quite a challenge to create the ability among the people involved to listen to performance issues and to realize that it is not bad to admit failures, mistakes, or strategic errors. A real problem exists when those signals are ignored and when the foundation continues to undertake a poorly constructed project.

Another focus of the discussion was external evaluation, i. e. how to use expert committees from the outside to bring new ideas into an institution and to break down the internal self-reflective nature that many foundations develop. The ability to get other foundations to cooperate does not only bring more resources to bear but it is also a sign that an idea, especially a risky idea, has some credibility.

An interesting point of discussion talked about in the workshop was the role of the media as a check on foundations. Media scrutiny of these institutions can be quite important but they often have a very poor understanding of how foundations operate. What to a journalist will sometimes look wasteful, e. g. a long-term project that is very slow in developing, can in fact be a very good idea.

The final part discussed in this area was that even with heavy emphasis on evaluation, a foundation has to protect innovation first so that the internal evaluative process will not discourage staff from taking well-considered risks or will even push them to change and alter the results of the process to make a project look better. When doing ongoing assessment, foundations have to be very careful not to create a "reign of terror" within their institution. At the same time the notion must be protected that most foundation projects are long-term, therefore an emphasis on assessment should not lead to an emphasis only on short-term or very concrete results.

6. *Personnel and staffing*

Everyone agreed that good staffing plays an important part in keeping an institution dynamic and vital. Among the challenges of recruiting good people into the foundation community is the fact that it is not big enough to enable people to develop a career and to provide opportunities to move them up through several ladders in an organization. Once people are on the staff, the question is how to keep them motivated and flexible. Work in the foundation world seems to be quite attractive and works like a magnet in keeping staff together. Therefore, it is important to develop recruitment strategies and personnel practices which would create a learning environment and an institution where people want to share their ideas, their insights, and their failures with one another.

7. Cooperation among foundations

The issue of cooperation among foundations came up at a crucial point during the discussions when someone pointed out that everything said in the workshop was very good but that there was very little sharing among foundations of their performance, of their failures, and of their evaluations. Foundations need to work together so that their work can actually be benchmarked within the field and that there can be comparisons made of how the costs of foundations relate to their activities. This led to a discussion about the need for smaller international meetings on this subject, the role of the Internet and other new technology as a way of sharing this information.

In conclusion, the whole discussion in the workshop turned out to be useful and provocative. Efficiency is obviously a more difficult concept to apply in the foundation sector. When applying it, foundations have to be sure that it does not inhibit the great quality of innovation. It is crucial for foundations to tackle this issue in order to be effective and to maintain credibility with the public.

Workshop V
Community foundations
Moderation: Shannon E. St. John

A *community foundation* is an independent charitable organization formed to collect and distribute donations from a wide range of donors to meet critical needs in a defined geographic area. It can serve cities or towns as a unit of geography; it can also serve states. But as this concept has spread outside the U.S. into other countries, it has often been adapted to the local culture, traditions and realities. In some cases *community foundations* have been developed to serve entire nations.

A *community foundation* is different from a private foundation where money comes from a single family or an individual person and which typically has a few areas of grantmaking interests. It is also different from a corporate foundation where a corporation has specific interests, often related to business interests. A *community foundation* is a vehicle to make philanthropy accessible to a wider variety of individuals and companies – a vehicle for philanthropy through which many individuals can create their own personal charitable fund in their own philanthropic interests.

The *community foundation* movement started in the U.S. about 80 years ago. Community foundations now exist in more than 400 communities across the country. They are the fastest growing segment of philanthropy in the U.S. In 1995 the total collected assets were about ten billion dollars. Outside the U.S. *community foundations* exist in Canada (about 70) and in the U.K. (about 40).

The first foundations in Canada were established soon after the first ones in the U.S. but only in the last decade has there been real growth. The concept also exists in Japan and Australia, and there has been some experimentation going on on the European continent in countries like Bulgaria, Slovakia and Russia.

This workshop primarily focussed on various practical items of starting and managing *community foundations*. A major issue addressed was whether *community foundations* could be vehicles to address the need to target private resources for the public good, not just in the U.S. but throughout the world. In particular, various aspects of starting a *community foundation* in Gütersloh as a possible model of this new philanthropic form to all of Europe were dealt with.

Social context and functions of *community foundations*

The role that non-profit and philanthropic organizations play is absolutely critical but is often overlooked. As we look at the changes taking place in our countries and communities, charitable organizations provide education for those who are socially, economically and politically disadvantaged and may even have an influence on government and the private sector to fulfill their obligations. They are important in strengthening the health and vitality of our communities and helping to effectively address problems at the local level.

The ability of the community to develop such an initiative depends on the commitment of resources and skills available at the local level. This requires investment in local non-profit organizations. In the U.S. philanthropy is considered as the venture capital of the social sector. Just as the economy needs capital so that it can expand and grow, the public welfare sector also needs this sort of capital to grow and develop, and philanthropy can play this role. Community foundations are particularly effective mechanisms at the local level to provide this venture capital and to empower a community to address local issues.

The four primary functions of a *community foundation* are:

1. Resource developer
A *community foundation* builds and manages resources for the long-term benefit of a community. This is usually in the form of a permanent endowment. It becomes a vehicle for individual citizens regardless of their economic means (also corporations, other foundations, or even governments) to pool their money and to channel it for the public good.

2. Donor service agent
A *community foundation* serves as a vehicle for donors with varied charitable interests. It can provide to individual donors a variety of services (grantmaking, financial management, additional resource development).

3. Grantmaker
In this role a *community foundation* responds to emerging and changing community needs through grantmaking, other community programs and leadership activities. It can assess the needs of the community, identify gaps and innovative approaches in a wide range of areas (such as culture education, environment or economic development, dealing with children, the elderly, the disabled, etc.). Through the many funds under the common umbrella it can target dollars to meet the community's most pressing needs and promising opportunities.

4. Community leader
A *community foundation* is an institution through which many non-profit organizations and also the private and government sectors can be convened to work toward a common goal. The foundation serves as a resource, an agent, an initiator and a catalyst in the local community. In this role *community foundations* can network with other area sponsors, they can stimulate public-private partnerships, they can bring worthy local projects to the attention of other national or perhaps international funders. Also, the board

of a *community foundation* can have a great impact not because of the money it spends but because of its ability to reach a broader group of community leaders.

Leadership, board development and staffing

The first ingredient of a successful *community foundation* is the same as the first ingredient for any other successful activity: *leadership*. Most successful *community foundations* in the U.S. have a visionary founder or founders. They come from all walks of life – attorneys, bankers, business people.

The second important element is the *board of directors*. The board of directors establishes and maintains a balance between a foundation's independence and its responsiveness to the community. The board must be representative of the community. When a *community foundation* is established, the entire community is invited to become philanthropists. In order for the entire community to feel a part of their *community foundation*, the foundation must encompass all the elements of the community. Those elements differ from community to community. In the U.S. one of the very important components is Afro-American representation on the board, however, in different communities representation means different things.

One question discussed in the workshop was if representatives of political parties, unions or churches should also be included in a *community foundation* board. Whereas in the U.S. people with specific political affiliations are usually not invited to become board members as the foundation wants to maintain its neutrality, in Canada and in the U.K. (where the state has more control) tripartite boards are common with people from the business, government (sometimes including politicians) and the non-profit sectors. Union representation can be very important in communities where industries with strong unions are located. Having people from churches on the board may be quite important as people of influence in the community are needed.

The board must be independent of any government, individual family or corporation. One of the ways independence is established is by counterbalancing representation. In fact, one probably ought to include key people from corporations and influential families, as well as key people from government agencies, although this may vary from foundation to foundation.

Representation is important but what is necessary is that the people chosen can attract donations, have significant knowledge of the community to make wise grants and also have enough financial management knowledge to be reliable trustees of the assets. Apart from the "wealthy representatives", you should also look at professional qualifications. It is good to have board members who are lawyers, accountants, and people with marketing experience who can help to promote the *community foundation*. There are many ways looking at characteristics of people to be selected. One aspect to be considered is age differences. Some very successful *community foundations* in the U.S. have deliberately involved younger people from the beginning, thus encouraging new generations to be interested in philanthropy.

The size of a *community foundation* board in the U.S. may vary between 8 and 40, the average is between 15 and 20. An important component for establishing independence is a good system of rotation of board members and officers. When you have terms of office, people can move on and off the board. So the foundation can adjust to the community and its changing needs. Although there are exceptions, the length of an office term tends to be three years whith a two-term maximum so that an individual board member can actually serve six years.

Of course, problems can arise when there is the first major rotation of a board. Therefore, it is wise to plan an orderly rotation system so that the entire initial board does not leave at the same time. However, the key element is that you cannot have renewal without some rotation of the board.

In many cases, the visionary founder will initially serve as *chair of the board* so that there is strong leadership in the beginning. The chair's job is to fully empower the working committees of the foundation (e. g. investment committee, grants committee, development committee), delegate responsibility to them and see to it that they do the best they can for the community. Because there is a temptation to keep the visionary founder as chairman, it is a job of human resource development to choose some potential future chairmen within the group of the initial board and look for opportunities to build their leadership capacity.

Apart from the board there are other ways to involve people in a *community foundation*. Many have *advisory committees or citizen groups*. Research in the U.S. shows that if a person volunteers time, he or she will give more money than a person who has not been involved on a personal basis. Once they are involved in voluntarism, then they will become donors as well.

The *staff* is a key component of the leadership of a *community foundation*. The experience in the U.S. shows that the earlier a foundation is able to hire a full-time professional and some support staff, the more quickly it will take off. As to the characteristics of a staff member, it would be helpful if the person had contacts in the community, knowledge of the community and also fundraising experience. However, it is most important that he or she has energy, intelligence and a passionate commitment to philanthropy. The executive needs to be someone who can work with many different types of people and who is able to juggle 100 balls in the air all at the same time. In the U.S. there are more women *community foundation* directors than men (as women tend to be good at consensus building, at nurturing and at communicating).

When hiring a new director, it is important to have a review process in place in order to be able to evaluate the performance of this person. There are times when the director does not work out and you need to be able to make a change. Therefore you need to be clear about the functions, the roles and responsibilities of that staff person and what they are going to be measured against for their performance. It is also good to have agreement between the full-time staff director and the board chairman, e. g. if the board chairman is not prepared to raise funds, the staff director has to.

The start-up period

For the start-up phase of a *community foundation* it is important to get wealthy people of the community involved. If you do not engage social leaders from the beginning, they will not join later. It is also necessary to motivate as many people as possible to get involved early on so that they will not get used to sitting back and watching the generosity of others.

When a *community foundation* is started, it is essential to have a strategic plan for growth and development. One part of the plan is how the administrative costs will be covered (during the first five years, and then long-term). The second is how the foundation is going to make grants: Where are financial sources to be found which would enable an immediate allocation of grants? The third question is: How is the *community foundation* going to build its endowment? Where will that money come from? The fourth is: What investments should be made for securing the growth of the endowment funds?

When creating a *community foundation*, it is wise to develop an administrative budget (staff costs, office costs, travel costs, etc.) for at least the first five years. In the U.S. to start up a community foundation, you need to budget a minimum of $100000 dollars per year. Sources of start-up money are typically private foundations (e. g. the Mott Foundation) or corporate foundations. Thus, a young *community foundation* does not have to worry about covering administrative costs for five years and can concentrate on raising endowment and grantmaking money.

Apart from providing administrative funds, private foundations can also assist and nurture *community foundations* in other areas during their start-up period. As long as those have not built up the resources for making their own grants, private foundations may provide dollars for programs and regranting (thus entrusting the *community foundation* to make decisions at the local level to target those grants toward needs in its community). Also, many private foundations in the U.S. have provided an invaluable service to *community foundations* by issuing a challenge, i. e. by providing a certain amount of dollars for the organization if it raises a matching amount or doubles the matching amount within its own local community. This provides a tremendous impetus for the local *community foundation* to approach donors to build its permanent resources. Finally, private foundations can offer assistance for professional development of the staff and the board of the new *community foundation* by allowing those board and staff members to visit other *community foundations* and to come to conferences in order to expand their view of the potential of their local *community foundation*.

A key in founding a *community foundation* is that there needs to be a strong sense of what its mission will be in the community. This has to be decided individually for each foundation. No mission statement can be given for the *community foundation* field as a whole but in general the mission will have to state how the community foundation will serve its key constituencies: donors, grantees (non-profit organizations) and the community as a whole. Also, the mission statements will define a geographic area. Your service area needs to have two key characteristics: to have a certain number of potential donors and to represent an area which fits the description of a community.

Sometimes there is tension between the idea of identifying potential donors in a certain area and the idea of what it is which encompasses a sense of community. The original model was that of a city (the Cleveland Foundation for Cleveland, Ohio). A second model includes a larger region (like the Triangle Community Foundation which encompasses a metropolitan area of three cities). A third model is a *community foundation* encompassing an entire state (e. g. the Delaware Community Foundation). In the U.S. there is a fourth model emerging: a core foundation encompassing either affiliates within its area or reaching out to affiliate geographic areas beyond its core area. In the U.S. there are two reasons for the trend towards larger geographic areas: The larger the geographic area the greater is the mass of potential donors. Also, there is a genuine desire on the part of many *community foundations* to serve those bordering areas that do not have the resources of their own to create a *community foundation*.

There is no general way of quantifying the term "right amount." In the U.S. there are a number of successful *community foundations* in towns with 100 000 inhabitants only. As to endowments, five million dollars are considered as the take-off point in the U.S. This is the point at which the growth of the *community foundation* can be guaranteed. One major element of "the right amount" is not numbers of people but community will: Is there enough commitment across the community to make this happen?

Future perspectives

A major ingredient for the success of *community foundations* is continuous re-invention and renewal. One of the most important avenues through which this can happen is the ability to learn from one another. This means a multiple-avenued interaction among *community foundations* across the world. Not only will emerging *community foundations* learn from older, more established foundations, but learning will go in the opposite direction as well. As new innovations are tried, new adaptations to cultures that have not previously had *community foundations* occur. The established foundations will be able to learn from the new experiments. Fortunately, the *community foundation* field is one in which this kind of interaction is part of the culture. In fact, in the *community foundation* field, imitation and "plagiarism" are an honorable art form. When the philanthropic impulse is unleashed, it will generate new and often unexpected levels of philanthropy for the public good.

Given the enthusiasm, energy and entrepreneurial spirit of Reinhard Mohn, Liz Mohn and Mark Wössner there was no doubt expressed in the workshop that the right amount for creating a *community foundation* was available in Gütersloh. However, it is necessary to decide very carefully how to proceed at the beginning so that the impetus will reach beyond this group. Otherwise, it will be difficult later on to get other people to take part.

Later on in the plenary session, Count Strachwitz expressed the view that there would be a great potential for starting *community foundations* in many German cities. The tradition of bequeathing something to one's home town by creating a foundation administered by local government would have to be rejuvenated. Today, this tradition has come to a standstill because the local authorities have not done a good job in running these foundations. If the existing foundations could be detached from the municipal authorities and become part of a non-governmental *community foundation*, this would definitely revitalize the notion of making a bequest to one's home town.

Conclusion

The responsibility of foundations today

Reinhard Mohn

Every society must have institutions which ensure that this society develops and evolves properly and does not stagnate. In order for a system's update to take place, we need independent organizations which provide impetus. When I see the innovative capacity of those in politics and government in this country, I have to say that the country is in dire need of foundations! Also, with regard to our democratic order, we need the commitment of citizens – not only their demands. We would like people to become involved in the thinking process and we would like mutual cooperation!

It is essential to recognize the significance of foundations within society and to take advantage of what they have to offer. Everyone realizes that change is necessary. However, not everyone realizes how this change is to be brought about. The catchword "operating foundation" can provide guidance. Foundations have the advantage of being independent – of not having to abide by rules and regulations nor by what has been handed down by tradition. We are in need of foundations which have the freedom to criticize and to develop creative ways of doing things. Assisted by these creative, operating foundations, we can set much in motion. I am grateful that I have been able to experience this! It is the reason why the Bertelsmann Foundation would like to awaken Germany to the idea of foundation work.

The growing importance of foundations for the development of society can no longer go unnoticed. We have met here at this forum to discuss the responsibility, objectives and methods of efficient foundation work. In these concluding remarks, I would like to cite what I feel are the most important results of our conference, to once again take a look at the questions concerning society today and, in conclusion, to give some examples of the work the Bertelsmann Foundation has undertaken.

Fostering creativity

The particular work assigned to a foundation is usually the result of the founder's observation of a given problem. He or she comes to the conclusion that a problem is worth examining more closely, that better solutions can be found than the existing ones, and that he or she would like to become committed to this cause. The personal attitude of the benefactor towards the foundation's objectives is crucial. I perhaps do not know which problem current in today's society presents the greatest difficulties in a global context; however, I do recognize certain problems and believe that I am able to solve some of them. Resulting from the professional experience I gained as an entrepreneur, my approach has always been to develop a problem-solving concept, to test it out in practice and then to learn from it. Those who are not willing to make mistakes cannot be innovative. One of the decisive factors for creativity within a foundation is the ability to admit and learn from mistakes. This is what enables a foundation to undertake the tasks which no one else – neither politicians nor public administrators – is willing to do. Many people have reflected on how to secure continuity in corporations and foundations. I am convinced that the best way of achieving this is to grant leeway for creative thought processes. Do not set goals for all eternity and do not let yourself get bogged down in old traditional patterns! The creativity which we would like to bring into the public sphere must also dominate in our foundations. There, open debate should be possible. As a way of delegating responsibility, give more creative leeway to your employees and staff members – creativity is something which has to be learned. The department head, managing director or member of the board who does not have the chance, at his or her workplace, to assume responsibility and initiate or organize projects, cannot *acquire* creativity. The freedom to err should become a basic principle of foundation work. Quite simply, nothing works without such a learning process!

Along these lines I would like to turn to the subject of "corporate culture," a topic of great importance also for foundations. From my experience as an entrepreneur, I was able to develop a new understanding of the objectives of the Bertelsmann Corporation. The intention was for each and everyone involved – not only the investors and managers but also the employees – to have the same chances for self-realization, for demonstrating initiative and voicing opinions at their workplace. It is a mistake to believe that confrontation supercedes cooperation as a principle of management. On the contrary, communication concerning common goals and endeavors is possible. Every individual employee, just like the entrepreneur, should be allowed the chance to become involved in organizing and creating. Only in this way can he or she find job satisfaction, which is positive not only for the individual but also for the company. In hierarchical organizations where decisions are made only at the top level of management, those working in the rank and file simply perform the duties assigned to them. The problems of our day cannot be solved in this way. We need more people who have learned to think and act creatively. The Bertelsmann company has fared well with the concept of corporate culture I initiated. Employees are able to identify with their jobs and are very creative. It seems obvious that a foundation could benefit from such an enterprise culture also. Personal satisfaction is not the only result – openness to innovation, flexibility and change are also fostered. It is in a certain sense a basis for progress in the system.

"Raison d'être" of foundations

When one reflects, as we have done, on the *raison d'être* of foundations, one thing becomes clear: foundations must justify themselves to the public through their actions and achievements. The Bertelsmann Foundation has developed and launched numerous model solutions and incentives for the development of our political and social system for the citizens of this country. We have not done this in opposition to politicians or the administration, rather, we have attempted, through dialogue, to build bridges and seek understanding of our concepts. Both politicians and administrators accept our competency in solving problems and in developing our social and political system. We are experiencing more and more mutual cooperation. These are visible achievements. It is important, in my opinion, for foundations to justify their actions through public reports. Detailed accounts of foundation activities should be published – after all, public funds are being used. And such accounts in the public arena are a self-evident fact! I can only hope that public corporate bodies in this country provide as detailed accounts as the Bertelsmann Foundation does. I am in favor of compelling the giant stock corporations to justify themselves publicly, too. After all, foundations must do the same.

Plurality and dialogue

We should not think that we all have to do things the same way. Look at the freedom of the press. It is solely due to the variety of efforts that freedom and progress have been secured. That is the way it should be for foundations, too. No foundation should claim it alone has the right answers. We have to listen to many different opinions and carefully weigh them up in order to determine which one is right. Individual personalities often influence foundations. This is the case in Germany and abroad. It results in a great variety of different opinions which, when coordinated as in the present symposium, result not in a synchronization of ideas but a forum for constructive dialogue. A learning process takes place. When there is a problem to be solved, it is not usually necessary for each individual to find his or her own solution to the problem. There is not a single problem existing which has not been solved at one time or another in some part of the world. We simply are not aware of it.

That is why cooperation is necessary and the exchange of ideas desirable! The international web of political, economic and social issues increasingly requires foundations to globalize their concepts and activities. We must not forget that the world we live in has manifold cultural possibilities. What we have to work on are the interim periods of transition within society, and that is not easy. At present we are greatly committed in eastern Europe, where the issue at hand *is* transformation. However it would not be a good idea for us to recommend that all periods of transition be treated in the same way. We don't want to harmonize, to destroy plurality. Competition of different systems is a source of innovation. We have to learn to debate at an international level. We have to confront other countries and other cultures and see what contributions they can make to ours. And the same is true for foundations. We must keep the different traditions and objectives of the many foundations in mind while continuing to communicate in order for new impetus to be gained.

Involving citizens in the community

An important social objective, in my opinion, is to carry over the spirit of philanthropy to the broader public. The community foundation is an outstanding outlet for philanthropy to become a part of living democracy. The concept of corporate culture is an equivalent to this in the business world. People want to be involved. They should be allowed to participate, to identify with the community and to make decisions. It would be erroneous to think that "democracy is defined through elections." No, democracy means that we may all participate. The community foundation is one component of effective and living democracy. One can learn about responsibility, solidarity, creativity and commitment. We are in urgent need of this! More than a hundred examples from the United States have shown that it is possible – that city-dwellers are willing to become involved in their towns – with action, commitment and money. The necessity to delegate and take on responsibility corresponds to our own self-image as do the human characteristics of wanting to help and wanting to commit oneself to a good cause. A community foundation can restore people with a sense of civic pride in their neighborhoods, communities and towns. We can pave the way for a new kind of relationship between citizens and communities. This form of foundation suits our present age. I would like to attempt to create such a model in our country. Do not think this is impossible in Germany. We simply have not tried it yet. We'll learn. And I'd like to begin the learning process in my own hometown.

Social problems and solutions

In this context I would like to cite some examples of key social problems and a few of the solutions which the Bertelsmann Foundation has developed. As I have already mentioned, the days when everything could just stay the way it was are over. It was once very useful to conduct business with regulations governing everything down to the smallest detail. Our age has taken on a new quality. We are participating in the global competition of systems. And, in this competition, we must be careful not to be among the losers. Is what we are doing in this country right? I believe that development is encouraged when we are somehow compelled to achieve something. Have we experienced enough pressure yet to spur us into action? Should we really continue to consider past traditions, customs and privileges as right and just – without criticism? Haven't we noticed that there is something wrong with much of the social order in society? Couldn't it be that our political system is also in need of rejuvenation? I'd like to cite a few examples:

Consider stagnation in the economy, consider the negotiations with the government and the collective bargaining partners in the field of social responsibility. Is that which we are experiencing in our country today – the uncertainty, the indecisiveness, the lack of consensus and resolution – an example of a well-balanced, progressive system?

Even the debates being conducted today, for example, on the responsibility of the bargaining partners in the autonomous negotiation of wages, do not impress me. I am in favor of dialogue but what is taking place at the moment simply lacks quality. I also have to question in this respect the development of our social and political system – has it been rejuvenated? Has it it kept abreast of the times? Are we really in a position to keep up with the global competition of systems? These are questions which are not easily taken up by political parties or professional associations, nor by public administrators. And unfortunately, hardly at all, by politicians.

How do you judge public administration? A great portion of our gross national product is consumed by public administration. Do you consider the share allotted to the state in Germany as appropriate? Is this right for our society?

The Bertelsmann Foundation has illustrated in numerous projects how the public sphere of responsibility can be managed more efficiently – namely, through the introduction of competitve practices similar to the ones employed within the economy. We can do the same in education, in the health services and in administration. By initiating achievement-oriented practices in the public sphere, we could save – as a safe estimate – approximately 80 billion DM per year. Have you heard anything said about these possible savings in public debates? At the moment we hear only about reductions being made in our social service programs, which at one time were models for the rest of the world. Nothing is said about the savings which could be made through a new orientation towards efficiency.

The Bertelsmann Foundation has developed many different problem-solving concepts. One example is in the area of municipal management. Through international research we were able to find ways for optimizing municipal management. We introduced a system of management comparison between cities. This has become an indispensable tool for city management. Even in the most difficult areas, such as the cultural services division of a municipality, it can be determined very precisely whether citizens' needs are being met and whether reform programs have had an impact or not. This is done with the help of performance-oriented criteria.

It is difficult to effect change. We have, however, started to make a move in this direction. It is perhaps characteristic of the present situation that the Bertelsmann Foundation, in collaboration with the Hans Boeckler Foundation, has initiated a project entitled "Co-determination and new corporate culture." The subject of co-determination will be looked at from all angles – the management point of view and the personal point of view – in terms of creativity and of productivity. In the final analysis, this is perhaps the result of the success we have had in our experiment with corporate culture.

I would like to take advantage of this opportunity to cite the following question which we have asked ourselves at the Bertelsmann Foundation: Why is it that in the family, in the economy, in politics and in society, the capacity for reaching a consensus is continually on the decline? It is becoming more and more difficult to reach decisions. This state of affairs is not the same everywhere in the world. Analyzing the example of New Zealand, you will notice that a consensus of values exists there which, for various reasons, is no longer at our disposal here. This could be one aspect of the social system which a foundation could reflect upon. The Bertelsmann Foundation attempts to elucidate these basic rules and principles of a culture and to draw conclusions. What has become clear to me is that the steps made in this direction can only become effective in the long term. When a deficit in our society becomes visible, however, it must be tackled! A foundation is one way of doing it.

In the fall of this year, the Bertelsmann Foundation will deal with the topic of schools. *School* is a dreadful subject, not because I disliked going, but because nothing is moving in this area. There is no innovation. How could that be with the hierarchical structures prevailing in our schools today? The Bertelsmann Foundation, for this reason, chose the title "Innovative school systems in an international comparison" for a prize it will award this year. The aim is to find *the* most innovative system for schools and school regulatory bodies.

Perspectives

We have provided many incentives for the rejuvenation of our present social and political system. We need, however, much more impetus in this country. It is my heartfelt wish that the thoughts and ideas of this symposium will be passed on to the public – through the foreign guests present here, by the statement made by President Herzog, and by this symposium itself. It is the democratic way and the most successful way. All we need to do is to channel sufficient energy into creating a third sector, one which can help eliminate inefficiency and stagnation and make change possible.

I have learned a great deal in the last few days. The meetings and debates have provided so much inspiration and food for thought that I have not yet finished absorbing it all. There is one statement, however, I would like to make at this time. We would like this international forum of ideas to be carried on. We would like to secure the importance of this third sector in society. We would like to inspire more people to become committed to democratic principles. We would like them to voice their opinions, share their ideas on how they think things should be done. In this way, we can catch up with the 'backlog' of our system, which has brought upon us the hopelessness, the difficulties, the indifference and the stagnation we see today. If we succeed in achieving this goal, we will have made both a political and an entrepreneurial contribution to efficiency.

Annex

The authors

Harvey P. Dale
Since 1977 Professor of Law, New York University School of Law, New York. Since 1996 Director, New York University School of Law, National Center on Philanthropy and the Law; since 1995 Chairman, Cornell University Council.

Ricardo Díez-Hochleitner
President, The Club of Rome, Madrid. Executive Vice President, Fundación Santillana, Madrid.

Joel L. Fleishman
President, The Atlantic Philanthropic Service Company, Inc., New York. Since 1994 Trustee, Brandeis University; since 1991 Director, Heyman Center for Ethics, Public Policy and the Professions, Institute of Policy Sciences and Public Affairs, Duke University; since 1980 Fellow, National Academy of Public Administration; since 1974 Professor of Public Policy Studies, Institute of Policy Sciences and Public Affairs, Duke University; since 1974 Professor of Law, School of Law, Duke University.

Rien van Gendt
Executive Director, Bernard van Leer Foundation, The Hague. Since 1996 Member of the Board of Directors, US Council on Foundations; since 1995 Chairman, Hague Club (Association of

European Foundation Directors); since 1995 Member of the Board of Directors, European Foundation Centre; since 1995 Deputy Chairman of the International Committee, US Council on Foundations.

Roman Herzog
President of the Federal Republic of Germany, Bonn/Berlin.

Mikio Kato
Executive Director, The International House of Japan, Tokyo. Since 1989 Member of the Board of Trustees, Ishizaka Foundation; since 1980 Advisor and Director of the Tokyo Office of the Aspen Institute of Humanistic Studies.

Craig Kennedy
President, The German Marshall Fund of the United States, Washington D.C. 1986–1992 President, The Joyce Foundation.

Reinhard Mohn
Chairman of the Board of Directors, Bertelsmann Foundation, Gütersloh.

Wolfgang H. Reinicke
Member of the Senior Research Staff, Foreign Policy Studies Program, The Brookings Institution, Washington D.C. Professor, School for Advanced International Studies, Johns Hopkins University; Fellow to the World Economic Forum, Davos.

Shannon E. St. John
Executive Director, Triangle Community Foundation, Durham/ North Carolina, USA.

Rüdiger Stephan
Secretary-General of the European Cultural Foundation, Amsterdam. 1978–1994 Director of the Division "International Understanding", Robert Bosch Foundation, Stuttgart.

Werner Weidenfeld
Member of the Board, Bertelsmann Foundation, Gütersloh. Director of the Center for Applied Policy Research, Munich; since 1987 Coordinator for German-American Cooperation, German government.

Mark Wössner
Chairman of the Board, Bertelsmann Corp., Gütersloh.

The participants

Robert d'Arcy Shaw	General Manager, Aga Khan Foundation, Genf
Marc Beise	Editior, Economics and Politics, Division, Handelsblatt, Düsseldorf
Ann Bernstein	Executive Director, The Center for Enterprise and Development, Johannesburg
Prof. Dr. John Brademas	Member of the U.S. Congress (1959–1981); President of New York University (1981–1992), now President Emeritus; National Endowment for Democracy; American Ditchley Foundation, New York
Ignatz Bubis	Chairman of the Board of Directors, Central Advisory Board for Jews in Germany
Leopoldo Calvo-Sotelo Ibáñez-Martín	Sekretary-General, Centro de Estudios Avanzados en Ciencias Sociales, Instituto Juan March de Estudios e Investigaciones, Madrid
Francis Charhon	Le Directeur Général, Fondation de France, Paris
Michael Cohen	Senior Adviser, The World Bank, Washington D.C.

Prof. Dr. Harvey P. Dale	Director, Program on Philanthropy and the Law, New York University, New York
John J. Deeney	Director, The Hong Kong-America Center, The Chinese University of Hong Kong
Dr. Warnfried Dettling	Journalist, former Undersecretary, Munich
Christine DeVita	President, Dewitt Wallace – Reader's Digest Fund Inc., New York
Dr. Ricardo Díez-Hochleitner	President, The Club of Rome; Executive Vice President, Fundación Santillana, Madrid
Dr. Peter Dittmar	Editor, Culture/The Arts, Die Welt, Berlin
Prof. Dr. Manfred Erhardt	Former Senator of Berlin; Secretary-General, Association of German Science Foundations, Essen
Lewis Feldstein	President, The New Hampshire Charitable Foundation, Concord
Suzanne L. Feurt	Program Officer, Charles Stewart Mott Foundation, Flint, Michigan
Prof. Joel L. Fleishman	President, The Atlantic Philanthropic Service Company Inc., New York
Shepard Forman	Director, International Affairs Program, The Ford Foundation, New York
Arthur W. Fried	Yad Hanadiv, Jerusalem
Dr. Rien van Gendt	Executive Director, Bernard van Leer Foundation, The Hague
Robert B. Goldmann	Europe Commissioner, Anti-Defamation-League, New York
Juan González-Palomino	Secretary-General, Fundación Ramón Areces, Madrid

Dr. Franz-Theo Gottwald	Board of Directors, Schweisfurth Foundation, Munich
Sir Ronald Grierson	Board of Directors, European Organization for Research and Treatment of Cancer, London
Dr. h.c. Johannes Gross	Journalist, Cologne
Dr. Günther Hadding	Bertelsmann Book Corp., Zierenberg
Dr. Ingrid Hamm	Vice President Media Division, Bertelsmann Foundation, Gütersloh
Vyvyan Harmsworth	Director, Corporate Affairs, Associated Newspapers Holdings Ltd., London
Manfred Harnischfeger	Vice President, Corporate Communication and Public Relations Division, Bertelsmann Corp., Gütersloh
Mrs. Randolph Hearst	Publisher, Hearst Books, New York
Prof. Dr. Roman Herzog	President of the Federal Republic of Germany, Bonn/Berlin
Dr. Rainer Hoffmann	Neue Zürcher Zeitung, Düsseldorf
Prof. Dr. James D. Hunter	Professor of Sociology and Religious Studies, University of Virginia, Charlottesville
Akira Iriyama	President, The Sasakawa Peace Foundation, Tokyo
Josef Janning	Deputy Director, Center for Applied Policy Research; Director of the Research Group on European Affairs, Munich
Dr. Roland Kaehlbrandt	Vice President, Division Communication and Public Affairs, Bertelsmann Foundation, Gütersloh

H. Peter Karoff	President, The Philanthropic Initiative, Boston
Mikio Kato	Executive Director, The International House of Japan, Inc., Tokyo
Craig Kennedy	President, The German Marshall Fund of the United States, Washington D.C.
Dr. Rudolf Kerscher	Board of Directors, Fritz Thyssen Foundation, Cologne
Wolfgang Koeckstadt	Chief Financial Officer, Bertelsmann Foundation, Gütersloh
Andreas Kottmeier	Managing Director, German Stroke Foundation, Gütersloh
Michael Kuntz	Economics Division, Süddeutsche Zeitung, Munich
Dr. Michael Maier	Editor-in-chief, Berliner Zeitung, Berlin
Rolf Möller	Former Undersecretary of State; Former Secretary-General, Volkswagen-Foundation, Hanover
Dr. Brigitte Mohn	Academic Marketing, USA Publishing, Bantam Doubleday Dell Publishing Group Inc., New York
Liz Mohn	President, German Stroke Foundation; Member of the Advisory Council, Bertelsmann Foundation, Gütersloh
Reinhard Mohn	Chairman of the Board of Directors, Bertelsmann Foundation, Gütersloh
Claudia von Monbart	Senior External Affairs Counsellor, World Bank, Paris

Lloyd N. Morrisett	President, The Markle Foundation, New York
Prof. Dr. Detlef Müller-Böling	Director, Center for Higher Education Development, Gütersloh
Dr. Horst Niemeyer	Former Secretary-General, Association of German Science Foundations, Essen
Hans-Christoph Noack	Editor, Economics Division, Frankfurter Allgemeine Zeitung, Frankfurt/M.
Dr. Marga Pröhl	Vice President of State and Public Administration Division, Bertelsmann Foundation, Gütersloh
Prof. Dr. Gisbert Freiherr zu Putlitz	Managing Director and Chairman of the Board, Gottlieb Daimler- and Karl Benz-Foundation, Ladenburg
Dr. Wolfgang Reinicke	Senior Research Associate, The Brookings Institution, Washington D.C.
Dirk Rumberg	Vice President Politics Division, Bertelsmann Foundation, Gütersloh
Michael Rutz	Editor-in-chief, Rheinischer Merkur, Bonn
Shannon E. St. John	Executive Director, Triangle Community Foundation, North Carolina
Prof. Dr. Ulrich Saxer	Professor of Journalism, University of Zürich
Alois M. Schader	Chairman of the Board, Schader Foundation, Darmstadt
Dr. Andreas Schlüter	Chief Executive Officer, Bertelsmann Foundation, Gütersloh

Rolf Schmidt-Holtz	President and CEO, CLT-UFA, Luxemburg
Henrik Schmiegelow	Director of Planning, Office of the President of the Federal Republic, Bonn
Gerd Schulte-Hillen	Chairman of the Managing Board, Gruner + Jahr Corp., Hamburg
Irene Schulte-Hillen	Chairman of the Board, Deutsche Stiftung Musikleben, Hamburg
Karl Ludwig Schweisfurth	Founder of the Schweisfurth Foundation, Munich
Franz Sommerfeld	Political Correspondent, Berliner Zeitung, Berlin
Dr. Rüdiger Stephan	Secretary-General, European Cultural Foundation, Amsterdam
Rupert Graf Strachwitz	Managing Director, Maecenata Management GmbH, Munich
Luc Tayart de Borms	Managing Director, King Baudouin Foundation, Brussels
Volker Then	Head of Department Cultural Orientation, Bertelsmann Foundation, Gütersloh
Collis O. Townsend	Executive Director, Delaware Community Foundation, Wilmington
Dr. Levin von Trott zu Solz	Head of Department Cultural Orientation II, Bertelsmann Foundation, Gütersloh
Thomas Veser	Journalist, Munich
Ulrich Voswinckel	Chairman of the Board, Körber Foundation, Hamburg
Hachirou Watanabe	Executive Director, Suntory Foundation, Osaka
Lord George Weidenfeld of Chelsea	Publisher; Chairman of the Board, Weidenfeld & Nicolson, London

Prof. Dr. Dr. h.c. Werner Weidenfeld	Member of the Board, Bertelsmann Foundation, Gütersloh; Director of the Center for Applied Policy Research, Munich
Bettina Windau	Head of Division, Public Libraries, Bertelsmann Foundation, Gütersloh
Dr. Mark Wössner	Chairman of the Board, Bertelsmann Corp., Gütersloh
Dr. Heimfrid Wolff	Former Vice President Economics Division, Bertelsmann Foundation, Gütersloh
Shaun Woodward	Partner, Sardens Partnership, Chipping Norton
Prof. Masakazu Yamazaki	Member of the Board of Directors, Suntory Foundation, Osaka
Prof. Dr. Michael Zöller	Professor of Political Sociology and Adult Education, University of Bayreuth, Bayreuth

Theses of the Bertelsmann Foundation

The growing importance of foundations for the development of society cannot be overlooked. Therefore, we would like to start an intensive dialogue on the responsibilities, objectives and methods of efficient foundation work.

How can we enhance our engagement as operative foundations? Which new forms of international cooperation can be realized? Which instruments will help achieve the foundations' objectives most accurately? These questions will be the focal point of the symposium "The Work of Operating Foundations: Strategies – Instruments – Perspectives".

The discussion about operating foundations will be centered around six topics:

1. Working methods of operating foundations

The foundation landscape is abundant and sophisticated. There are grantmaking foundations, foundations with a special political or public responsibility, and operating foundations. In practical foundation work, grantmaking and operative methods often mix. Nevertheless, the work of an operating foundation is characterized by the following criteria. It
- has clearly defined instruments at its disposal;
- generates, tests and implements innovative strategies for solving societal problems it takes up;
- combines scientific or academic analysis with the innovative and creative potential of practical experts, entrepreneurs etc.;

- organizes the competition of innovative suggestions and acts as an agent of social innovation;
- independently launches and shapes projects to this end;
- cooperates systematically with competent external partners;
- works achievement-oriented according to the example and methods of the US American think tanks;
- stimulates innovations in government, administration and society;
- generates pressure to reform through active public relations work, relying on cooperation and continued exchange with institutions of the state or the public sector in general;
- is able to forge links between sponsors and a sensible use of their means.

2. Challenges for progress in society

- Foundations are charitable institutions. They have to decide independently how to meet the resulting societal obligations;
- They do not compete for economic success but for the best ideas.
- Foundations support government and society in their effort to comply with increasing demands for efficiency, systemic adaptation, and flexibility.
- At the same time, foundations have to face competition.
- Foundations develop solutions as models for current problems, and stimulate change in political and societal systems. They work as the motor of development within society.
- Foundations operate as early warning systems for problems to be expected and their significance for the future.
- The concentration of creativity and flexibility prepares operating foundations particularly well for innovations.
- Foundations as they see themselves incorporate the ideal of responsibility of citizens for the community as well as the ideals of decentralization, self-determination and subsidiarity.
- Foundations act as mediating structures between individual per-

spectives, social needs and state-imposed obligations. They shape the contours of political culture.
- The global interchange in today's world leaves foundations with new challenges. They can participate in a division of labor with governments and international organizations and become competent actors in new public policy areas. This includes new tasks of mediation and 'translation' across social and political boundaries.
- Foundations are predisposed to act in such a way because the solution of many problems is linked to long-term cultural processes.
- With their work, foundations can strengthen the links between citizens and their community. A prominent example of this are the community foundations in the United States. They can be a stimulating model for Germany, especially on a local level.

3. Governance of Foundations

- Structures of governance in foundations have to ascertain the independence and accountability of foundations.
- The governing structures of a foundation work in the most successful way by combining focus and flexibility in a long-term perspective.
- Foundations particularly require this governance structure for their strategic decision making. This structure has to balance the representation of family or company members and members of public life.
- Governance structure and strategic decisions have to assure the long-term innovative capacity of a foundation.
- At the same time decisions have to be made so as to guarantee the continued work in the fields of focus for which the foundation has acquired competence and in which its work can be most effective.

4. Organization, cooperation, evaluation

Organization
- To comply with high demands, foundations have to have an appropriate inner organization.
- Possible structures of organization are for example: departments and/or divisions with specific areas of projects; project teams spanning several departments.
- Dovetailing departments that work on projects and contents on the one hand with panels (administration and public relations) on the other increases efficiency.
- When determining staff and management structures, it is advisable to emphasize creativity and flexibility with respect to the innovative character of operative work in foundations.
- The work on projects has to be accompanied by an appropriate system of reporting that allows for budgeting and budget control. It is the prerequisite for coordinating extensive and often internationally-oriented projects.

Cooperation
- Cooperation among foundations serves the aims of achieving rationality, effectiveness and evaluation of foundation work.
- The concentration of knowledge and experience increases the effectiveness of foundation work.
- For the sake of self-interest, cooperations create comparative standards of internal action, which reduce the self-referential character of foundation work and assist in distinguishing optimal strategies to achieve project results.
- Cooperation provides a mechanism of accountability built into the projects, which helps to improve project control prior to public assessment.
- Possible forms of cooperation are: common teams; single projects in a spirit of partnership organized by the foundation; networks of partners at the same level; academies; specific instruments for public relations; and further education.

Evaluation
- Operating foundations need reliable methods of evaluation and decision structures based on them.
- Work in foundations needs continuous examination of the main emphases with respect to choice, objectives and performance regarding their societal relevance.
- Evaluation aims at discovering and enhancing the efficiency of the foundation's structures and its innovative potential.
- Evaluation equally aims at conveying the results of the work.
- Checking the success by evaluation can be achieved by the foundation's employees using internal structures of reporting and supervision, or by external controlling by third parties.
- Evaluation can help to discover new topics and to maintain the foundation's innovative potential.

5. Advantages of cooperation among foundations

Globalization
- The international interdependence of political, economic and societal relations calls for an increasing globalization of thinking and activity also within foundations.
- Foundations can enhance their efficacy in scope and contents by joining forces and forming networks.

Joining forces
- Cooperation aims at
  - combining financial resources,
  - joining know-how,
  - coupling experience in organization,
  - covering regionally diverse topics in different areas of the world,
  - distributing models for solving problems,
  - increasing efficiency to shape processes in society,
  - carrying out projects to compare cultures,
  - intensifying pressure to realize innovative models.

- It is particularly important for operating foundations to cooperate with grantmaking foundations. Cooperating with operating foundations, the sponsoring foundations encounter well-established management structures that are constantly being supervised. They can use the formers' experience in evaluation and project management.
- Operating foundations forge links between sponsoring foundations on the one hand and definition and fulfillment of their objectives on the other.

Efficiency
- The amount and scope of international cooperation are a benchmark for the success of the work done in operating foundations. Acquiring external funds is a proof for a sound choice of priorities.
- International networking among foundations facilitates comparison of societal problems and solutions across boundaries and cultures, and permits division of labor.
- International cooperating foundations can influence governments, economies, and public or scientific international organizations more thoroughly.
- International cooperation among foundations improves the efficiency of projects that require local branches in specific countries or regions. Branches consume financial and administrative resources, and their work needs to be organized for the long term rather than on a project by project basis.
- Since cooperative projects have strong effects on the corporate identity of foundations, cooperation requires common strategies for appearance in public.

6. Incentives for foundation commitment

- Foundations are unable to solve all societal problems; they cannot reform society as a whole.
- However, they can initiate developments.

- Legal requirements and tax regulations have a strong influence on the decision to establish foundations. Yet, they can also prevent commitment in foundations. A legal system that encourages potential sponsors can foster assuming societal responsibilities by the private sector.
- Based on the principle that "property imposes duties," citizens willing to donate could be encouraged by public incentives to increase their contributions towards the innovative development of society.
- Existing foundations can serve as examples and provide operative services to contribute to this motivation. This way, the first step towards philanthropic work can be facilitated for potential donors.
- Foundations initiate or rather promote the establishment of new foundations.

7. Questions

Against this background a number of questions as to the work and cooperation of foundations may be raised:
- How can operating foundations determine the need for action in society?
  - How do foundations discover the need for action in specific problem areas?
  - Which values and principles do they use for orientation?
  - How do they define appropriate objectives?
  - Which methods and instruments do they select for realizing projects?
  - How do they assess their success and according to which principles do they evaluate their entire project work?
- What instruments do operating foundations use to pursue their objectives beyond single projects?
- How can foundations maintain strategic continuity in the long run?
- Which governance structure is most apt to this purpose?

- How can their activities and their inner organization be optimized?
- How can budgeting and continuous budget control be enhanced?
- What does international cooperation among foundations contribute to the efficiency of foundation work?
- Which forms of cooperation have proven successful?
- How can external funds extend the scope of action for foundations?
- How can operating foundations make their work more transparent to the public?
  - How can the aims of foundations be presented optimally in public?
  - How can objectives and results of project work be presented intelligibly?
  - How can strategies of economic and personnel management tested by foundations be conveyed to the public sector?
  - How can the function of policy consulting be enhanced?